The world of
CATS

The world of
CATS

by John Montgomery

Hamlyn
London·New York·Sydney·Toronto

Published by
The Hamlyn Publishing Group Limited
London · New York · Sydney · Toronto
Hamlyn House · Feltham · Middlesex · England
© copyright 1967 Paul Hamlyn Limited
Reprinted 1970, 1971, 1972
Printed in Italy by Arnoldo Mondadori Editore · Verona
ISBN 0 600 00635 2

Contents

Are You a Catman?

In his novel *The Waters Under the Earth* author John Moore suggested that household pet owners may be divided into two camps — dogmen and catmen. With three cats in his Gloucestershire farmhouse, he was unashamedly pro-cat.

A dogman, he said, likes having tails wagged at him, wants to be looked up to, and tends for that reason to be quite a good leader. A catman, on the other hand, is made slightly uncomfortable by spaniel eyes and devoted tail thumpings. Dogmen seem to prefer the outdoors, adventure, jungles, deserts, and are attracted by the army. Little is heard of cats in army officers' messes or barracks, but a ship's company usually includes a cat. Simon, the famous cat on board H.M.S. *Amethyst*, was wounded in the River Yangtse battle and died at the early age of two, mourned by his mess-mates.

Mr Moore's theory is that dogmen drink whisky rather than wine, play golf instead of cricket, adore rugby football, and smoke pipes rather than cigarettes. A typical dogman strides over the desert wearing shorts, puffing away at his pipe, followed at a respectful distance by a batman or some devoted chap who happens at the moment to be a substitute for his dog. It is a fact that dogs attach themselves to troops, especially on the march. But as soldiers now move mainly in armoured troop carriers or tanks or by air, more dogs are staying at home.

Napoleon liked dogs and movingly described a cur sitting by its dead master on the field of Waterloo, but he is said to have broken into a cold sweat when a kitten approached him. Lord Kitchener of Khartoum owned several dogs and liked to be photographed in full dress uniform with an adoring spaniel lying at his feet, but he hated cats, which made him sneeze. His Commander-in-Chief, Lord Roberts of Kandahar, V.C, also loathed cats, which made him shiver when they went near him. The fact is that dogs usually obey orders, but cats simply won't be commanded. Is that why dogs attach themselves to men of action like the late Donald Campbell and air ace Douglas

Are you a catman or a dogman — or both?

Bader? But not all heroes are dogmen. Sir John Smyth, V.C, the chairman of the Victoria Cross and George Cross Association, owns four cats and has written two cat books. Wing-Commander Guy Gibson, V.C, hero of the Ruhr dam-busting exploit of the Royal Air Force in 1943, had an 'all-swimming and all-flying' cat called Windy who, he recorded, 'had put in more flying hours than most cats'. And another famous British airman, Wing-Commander Geoffrey Cheshire, V.C, kept a Siamese cat called Harem at his station. Harem was also known as 'Fighter Pilot' and 'The Killer', because of his ability to kill mice.

If there isn't anything military about cats, is there something about them that attracts writers and poets? Walter de la Mare, William Cowper, W. H. Davies, T. S. Eliot and C. Day Lewis can be numbered among the catmen, as were Victor Hugo, Balzac, Mark Twain, Dumas and Samuel Butler. Hilaire Belloc, although a downland walker, sailor, and hearty carouser, wrote an essay called *Conversation with a Cat* which contains the line 'At least you do not take us for gods, as do the dogs'. And Swinburne called his cat a 'stately, kindly, lordly friend'. Can it be true that dogmen need affection and admiration while catmen prefer to care for others? Abraham Lincoln was certainly a catman, and he never sought any sort of admiration.

Important cat people in our times include a number of creative writers and artists, such as Picasso, Olivia Manning, Cecil Woodham-Smith, Raymond Chandler, Elizabeth Jane Howard, Gavin Lyall, Doris Lessing, Pamela Hansford Johnson (Lady Snow), Dame Margot Fonteyn, James Mason, Gavin Lambert, Beverley Nichols, Noel Coward, film director Anthony Asquith (President of the Cat's Protection League), novelist Margery Sharp, Anna Neagle, Truman Capote, Paul Gallico, Enid Blyton, Robert Graves, Sir Compton Mackenzie and Patricia Highsmith, who dedicated a book to her pet mouser.

Cat lovers aren't necessarily anti-dog. 'I don't dislike them,' said John Moore. 'Although the tail-wagging fawning kind makes me slightly embarrassed. I'd like to have a whippet, which is one of the loveliest things that run, but I don't think my cats would approve. I own three cats and that is enough. Each is different and idiosyncratic. You can go on learning

Cats and writers. Dr Johnson and his famous cat, Hodge

The French author Colette and one of her many friends

about them as long as they live.'

Rudyard Kipling wrote a story called *The Cat that Walked by Itself*, telling how the dog and the horse both gave up their independence in return for food and safety, while the cat made a bargain with man to catch rats and mice for him and to be kind to children. In return, the cat was to receive milk and a place by the fireside, but otherwise he was to remain completely independent of the human race. He has remained independent ever since.

One of the most famous cats of history was Dr Johnson's Hodge, who 'doted on oysters'. In her later years, Florence Nightingale would never travel without her cats, and at one time she owned about sixty, all large Persians, named after famous men of the time like Disraeli, Gladstone and Bismarck. Other cat-lovers of the past have included Wordsworth, Shelley, the Brontës, Carlyle, Charles Dickens, Thomas Hardy, Thomas Gainsborough, and Sir Joshua Reynolds. But Brahms hated cats and sat at his window in Vienna shooting at them with a bow and arrow.

Can one like both cats and dogs equally? Actor Dirk Bogarde has a cat and a dog and hates being parted from either. The satirist J. B. Morton, 'Beachcomber' of Narkover fame, likes a dog for long walks but wants a cat sitting by his fireside. Who but 'Beachcomber's' dog could welcome his master home 'by tearing round and round the lawn until he was exhausted'? But perhaps the most famous combined catman and dogman was Sir Winston Churchill, who lavished affection on all animals. His marmalade cat sat under the table at wartime cabinet meetings, solemnly washing its paws, and the great man is said to have wept when his poodle Rufus died. You must be a true animal lover to care equally for such widely different kinds of creatures.

Many leaders of men, kings and statesmen, have loved cats. Mohammed was said to have taken a pair of scissors to cut away the hem of his cloak before standing up, rather than disturb his sleeping cat.

Stanley Baldwin, Prime Minister of Great Britain in the twenties and thirties, was surely a dogman, and his opponent Ramsay Macdonald owned a terrier, but most modern English politicians seem to prefer cats. Harold Wilson's Nemo, oddly named after a boat in the Scilly Isles, could claim

Cats and statesmen. Winston Churchill stops to talk to the ship's cat

Harold Wilson and family, including Nemo

to be the first feline to live at 10 Downing Street since Churchill and his marmalade friend moved out, although there is now also a dog there.

Nemo is Siamese, eats tinned food and sleeps next to the radiator in the bathroom. And if he didn't actually own a cat while he was Prime Minister, Sir Anthony Eden has certainly kept one in retirement. A journalist who went to interview him found a cat and a litter of kittens in the coat cupboard.

Other English politicians who prefer cats to dogs include Anthony Greenwood (with three) and Douglas Jay, while Lord Snow, no doubt influenced by his novelist wife, has Siamese mousers as supporters on his crest.

In London the Home Office has its own black Manx named Pete, officially presented by the Governor of the Isle of Man. Part of the establishment, Pete is paid half-a-crown a week for food, but the cost of living is rising and cat lovers will agree that this is hardly enough to feed him. Will Pete one day go on strike?

Lord Butler, as a former Home Secretary, contributed to the expense of having the previous Home Office cat buried in a flower-covered coffin. Civil servants in formal clothes attended the funeral. It is said that an earlier Home Office cat, named Emily, had been found in the street by a charwoman who took it to Whitehall, where it was adopted by the department.

Cats are certainly *in*. Not that dogs are out, or likely to be, but each year the R.S.P.C.A., Blue Cross, P.D.S.A, and other animal welfare societies report a fall in canine pet figures and a rise in the number of pet cats, due to changing living conditions. While some householders admit 'No children', many local housing authorities rule 'No dogs'. As more flats rise where there were once houses and cottages with gardens, so fewer tails wag. It is difficult enough to smuggle even a small dog into restaurants and supermarkets these days, and he must nearly always be kept on the lead because of traffic. Urban dogmanship is full of difficulties. But cats prowl on their own and are content to sit at home and wait for the sound of your latchkey in the door.

Cats are certainly less trouble than dogs, and are equally affectionate in their own way. They require less attention and little organized exercise, need no licence, are cleaner in their

Kitt and kittens. Eartha Kitt is definitely a catwoman

Lunchtime at the Robert Graves house

habits, cheaper to feed, don't bark, can be taken on trains and buses in baskets, and seldom bite the postman or milkman.

We have all heard of a dog's life, and dirty dogs, and we know the expression 'It shouldn't happen to a dog', but is it mere coincidence that gorgeous girls are not only known as ladies, dames, broads, birds, dolls, bunnies — and even women — but are, in this often tough, money-grabbing, commercial and too often unattractive world, known also by the soft, provocative, and delightful expression — *pussy cats*? And don't forget that Mr Cruft, the organizer of the world famous dog shows, always kept a cat.

John Moore, who made the distinction between cat and dogmen, with Candy

Below: Italian Prince Vittorio Massimo with some of his feline subjects

Peter Cook and friends

Columnist Cassandra (the late Sir William Connor) with Smokey Joe

Claudia Cardinale surrounded by her cats and cat pictures.   Right: Ursula Andress, who starred in *What's New Pussycat?*

When the Cat Was Divine

The cat family can be traced back about 40 million years. The domestic cat as we know it is a close relative of the African wild cat (*Felis libya*) which is still common in Africa and parts of South West Asia and which interbreeds freely with the modern domestic cat. The markings of the African wild cat are similar to those of our own tabbies. In Britain the wild cat (*Felis silvestris*) is now found only in Scotland, where its numbers are increasing.

Cats are found in various species throughout the world, except in the Australian region, Madagascar and the oceanic islands. They did not arrive in South America until almost a million years ago. The United States has seven species of natural cat, including the lynx, jaguar, ocelot, margay, and the jaguarondi, but the last four are rare, being found along the Mexican borders of Texas, New Mexico and Arizona.

The domestic cat is said to have been first reported in Egypt in about 2,500 B.C, and an effigy at Beni Hassan, discovered about two centuries later, revealed that it was known by the name of *Mait*, the feminine form of *Mau*, a word supposed to have been derived from the sound of mewing.

The old Egyptian name for a tom cat was a *Gib* or *Gilbert* or *Gibbe-cat* (with a hard G) and this term has persisted in certain forms in parts of Northern England and Scotland, where it is still known. It is possible that the Romans brought it to England. It seems to have applied only to old, serious cats. Thus, Shakespeare makes Falstaff say, 'I am as melancholy as a Gib-cat'.

Whenever an Egyptian temple was dedicated to the sun, an image or symbol of a cat was prominently placed inside. Ancient and modern legends agree that the Egyptians believed that a divine spirit rested inside the effigy. Not only cats were mummified when they died, but also mice — presumably to provide food for the cats in the after-life.

The ancient Chinese believed they could tell the time by gazing into a cat's eyes. But the Chinese did not tame and domesticate the cat until

From Ancient Egypt, a sacred cat in bronze

about A. D. 300, when they called it *Mao* or *Miu*.

No one really knows when tame cats were first introduced to Britain, but it is likely that Phoenician traders brought them on their sailing boats when they visited Cornwall to trade and barter for the tin which was mined there.

During the Middle Ages in Europe the cat had a very unfortunate time. His previous history as a divine creature and the fact that he was by superstition mixed up with both good and evil spirits, made him an animal to be regarded with fear and dread. He became the victim of appalling sacrifices and cruelty, and was connected with Black Magic and witchcraft. Witches were believed to turn themselves into cats, and many innocent women were burned to death with their pets, having 'confessed' under torture. Black cats were picked out for persecution as being the familiar of the Devil. It was only with the growth of rational thinking that the cat became a fireside pet. In France cats were publicly burned as sacrifices until the practice was forbidden by Louis XIII.

Towards the end of the Wars of the Roses a nobleman named Sir Henry Wyatt was imprisoned in the Tower of London. Each day a cat visited him in his dungeon, bringing a pigeon which he had caught on Tower Hill. The jailer was persuaded to cook the birds for the prisoner's supper, and it is said that Sir Henry and his friend shared the meal. There is a portrait of him in the National Portrait Gallery, and next to him is the cat, carrying a pigeon.

When you look at some of the handsome pedigree cats in this book you will be surprised to learn that the first cat show was not held in Britain until 1871, when the Crystal Palace was hired and several hundred cats were put on show. From then onwards it became a popular annual event. With Queen Victoria's patronage of the R.S.P.C.A. and the interest shown in all animals by Queen Alexandra, the beautiful Princess from Denmark, people began to think more about animal welfare, and cat and dog breeders began experimenting in producing different breeds and varieties, concentrating on beauty, dignity and perfection of character. Today the cat is at last respected and admired, if not actually worshipped, as it was in Egyptian times.

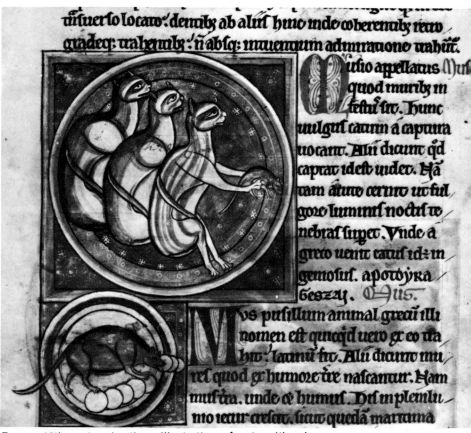

From a 13th century bestiary, illustration of cats with mice

From a 20th century window, a modern symbol of domestic bliss

Cats Have 'It'

One of the most romantic personalities of the 1920s was the novelist Elinor Glyn, the creator of 'It' — the mysterious quality of allure which attracted men. You either had 'It' or you didn't. People asked — *'What is "It"? How do you acquire "It"? Have I got "It"?'*

Miss Glyn went to Hollywood and became the high priestess of a cult which swept America and Europe. She taught the great Rudolph Valentino how to kiss his film heroines on the palms of their hands, and she chose red-haired actress Clara Bow as the perfect 'It' girl of the roaring twenties. Miss Glyn lay on the floor on a leopard skin rug and everything she said was reported in the world's press. A cat lover, she looked strangely feline. Beverley Nichols later described her as having 'the eyes of a cat, the purr of a cat, and at times the claws as well'.

Miss Glyn was shrewd. 'Cats have more natural "It" than most humans,' she said.

Today, of course, they are simply more naturally 'With It' than humans.

Novelist Elinor Glyn, shown above with two Persians, said that cats have more natural 'it' than humans. What else would you call the mysterious appeal of her pets and the other lively faces shown on these pages.

Good Companions

If brought up together, cats will be friendly with most other animals. A well-run home often contains a dog, a cat and a budgerigar, and they all get on perfectly well together. There is no reason why domestic animals should fight, except the fear of losing their place in the home. If you can persuade them that they are perfectly safe and that providing they behave themselves they will all have equal status, there is no reason why your cat should not be friendly with a whole variety of animals and birds. Jealousy can be overcome by proving to your pet that he is at home, and is cared for. That really is all he wants. If he is sure of this he is quite willing to share the house with your Boxer dog, or allow the chickens to roam around the farm unmolested, or play with a tame rabbit on the lawn, or even take up with stranger pets like — believe it or not — mice.

What's this, it's moving!

I wonder if it bites?

This is what I call friendship

And then I got him with a right cross to the jaw!

A territorial dispute

Strange bedfellows. Kitten and Crow are such good friends that they eat off the same plate and share the same bed

Whoever started the rumour that dogs and cats are enemies?

I'll have to be quicker next time

Kittens

A lovely thing it is to own one's own first kitten — soft and furry, curled comfortably before one's fireplace — or elusive with that hint of mystery, stalking the fallen leaves, lying in wait for birds and mice, peeping around the plants ready to surprise an unsuspecting mistress on her morning tour of the garden.

All cats are lovely, whether born in catteries of the élite or in a humble kitchen. Over each we hold the power of life and death, a literally awful thought. Sometimes our friendship with them is so close that the veil between human and animal intelligence wears very thin — then one experiences the supreme thrill of keeping a cat, or perhaps allowing oneself to be owned by a cat.

First of all we see, perhaps, one kitten amongst a litter that must be ours. That one and no other. Harden your heart and turn away if you are not prepared to sacrifice a little of your time and freedom, for which you will be more richly rewarded than you deserve, then do not purchase that kitten. Let another, who is prepared to bestow the small price exacted, have the pleasure and joy it will bring.

From *Your Cat and Mine*
by Catherine Manley

The garden is an exotic jungle

When you're young everything's exciting — even a wrinkle in the rug

All cats are lovely when they're kittens

Hide and Seek among the house plants

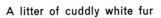

A litter of cuddly white fur

Mr Cat

Catless and alone was my status in the summer of 1943. Deborah, my delightful Maltese who had been living with my parents in Winchester, had been run over by an automobile and killed. Guiltless of cat hairs was my Manhattan apartment and there wasn't a scratch or a scar on the upholstery. There were no imperious morning and nightly calls for attention and feeding. There was no cat in my life, save the memories of the many whom I had known and cherished since early childhood. In short, I wanted the soft affection, the alert mind, the beauty and homeliness of a cat about the house.

With this in mind, I called a friend then scouring the East Side pet shops on behalf of her husband who had suddenly developed a passion for small fish. I said I thought she *might* just add a glance about for a Persian kitten, one that might enliven and make my life savourable again.

Several days later, entering a Second Avenue emporium, Ruth heard vague noises of unmistakable kitten origin. After first conscientiously attending to her husband's affairs, Ruth made discreet inquiries and was promptly ushered to the back of the shop by the proprietor who produced four tiny balls of fur.

'I sensed at once,' she told me later that evening, 'that my search was over.' I thanked her politely but cautiously and said that I would pass by in a day and take a look.

What a likely and hapless fool was I! You simply do not 'take a look' at kittens when the need for cat companionship was as strong as mine. The next afternoon, on the fateful day of August 2, 1943, I entered the shop and asked if I too might see the kittens in residence. I too was led to the back, shown a small chicken coop and treacherously left to myself.

Four little Persians poured out, their bright eyes exploring the world. Four little Persians, but one only looked in my direction. I extended a tentative finger and two soft paws clung to it. There was a contented sound of purring, I suspect on both our parts.

Was there any decision to make? Besides, wasn't this the handsomest

How could you choose which one to take home?

With tail erect, he leads the way

and certainly the most intelligent and friendliest? Besides, hadn't *he* chosen *me*? Indeed, the search was over.

My kitten's father was a handsome auburn to whom I was then presented. Father was most indifferent to the whole transaction and cared little about the fruit of his dalliance and obviously less about me. Mother I never met, as she was kept at home with a lone kitten to keep her busy.

I carried my purchase off in a cardboard carton carefully punctured with air holes. As the proprietor bade me goodbye, I thought I spied a look of quiet satisfaction in his eye as though he had had no doubts of the charm of his kitten.

En route home in a taxi, the box let out some muffled cries. The cab came to a stop and my driver turned round with an accusing look which I hastened to allay.

'A cat!' he marvelled, 'You've got a cat in the box! Noises! I kept hearing noises and I looked everywhere and I couldn't see nothin'. A cat! I thought I was nuts.'

As both of them had quietened down, the cab continued on its way and in a few minutes we swung off Madison Avenue west into 55th Street and stopped at *our* door. (Already I thought of it as his and mine). *Ours*, then, was a converted, five–storey Victorian brownstone with a doorway hidden between two shop windows. Each floor of the house had but two apartments on it and ours was on the top.

As I entered the lift, carefully balancing my carton, the neighbour with whom I shared the fifth floor joined me. When she heard the soft kitten mewing, she spoke in French rapidly (perhaps they don't speak in any other way) but I caught enough to learn that she adored cats and kittens and wanted to meet mine. Could she come in?

'Of course.'

We entered my apartment together and when I had loosened the cord, the top of the carton was pushed up by a little head. I set the box on the floor, tilting it a bit so that in a moment a very perky kitten emerged.

'May I pick him up?'

She could.

'*Un chat. Un chat persien! Mademoiselle ou Monsieur?*'

She determined by lifting its tail, despite indignant yowls at the other end.

She nodded: '*Monsieur Chat.*'

And so that is how Mr Cat came to be named.

Mr Cat was six weeks old when I got him, so his official birthday is June Sixteenth. At this moment of writing it is more than sixteen years later and he is still the same — alert, lively, companionable and beautiful. He is larger, of course, and older, but not obese in the way of some altered males. On that August afternoon, when I fetched the pan and a bowl of milk, it was Mr Cat himself and not I who led the way to the bathroom. With tail erect, it was the first of several thousand pussycat parades. May they never stop!

From *Mr Cat* by George Freedly

Too Many Kittens?

Many people think it cruel to 'doctor' or 'neuter' cats but this is not true. It is usually kinder. A neutered tom cat will be unable to father kittens and is disinclined to fight, is cleaner, does not smell, and will not increase the population of unwanted kittens. Toms should be taken to a veterinary surgeon or clinic for neutering between the ages of three and six months, unless of course you are seriously considering breeding cats. Even after six months, a cat can be 'doctored' at any time. The operation on the male takes only a few minutes and has no effect except to make him more contented, relaxed and home-loving. It is performed while he is under an anaesthetic and it is painless. Don't feed him before you take him to the vet or clinic because if he has eaten first the anaesthetic might make him sick.

A similar operation on the female, or queen, is a little more difficult because it requires an internal operation. But it is still simple and painless. Clinics seldom undertake it, but your vet will probably wish to keep the cat overnight. Don't feed her on the evening before you take her. Four months old is the ideal age, but in fact she can be of *any* age when it is done, even six or seven or more years. If she has been giving birth to kittens all that time she will probably be very grateful for the relief. Some people believe it is kinder to allow the queen to have at least one litter of kittens before she is operated on, but this really depends on what kind of cat she is and what *you* plan to do with the kittens when they are born. It is hardly right to allow a cat to bring kittens into the world if you are going to destroy them at birth. From every point of view, it is humane to regulate the cat population in some way. In Britain alone over half-a-million unwanted cats are destroyed every year, and the figure for the United States must be something like five or six million — a dreadful mass slaughter of the innocent which is quite unnecessary.

In ten years the average unspayed queen will produce over 100 kittens, whose immediate progeny is over 1,400.

Promiscuous breeding can cause great misery. The only certain way of preventing continuous litters year after year is for the queen to be spayed.

In Britain all the leading animal welfare societies recommend that cats of both sexes should be neutered. The value of a cat is actually increased by the operation. A record was kept of the kittens born to a queen between the years 1949 and 1961. In twelve years she gave birth to 102 kittens, but it didn't end there. During the same twelve years her 80 female kittens gave birth to 1,000 more. Therefore, between 1949 and 1961 a single cat and her offspring, because they were not neutered, produced at least 1,403 cats, many of which must have been unwanted and were probably turned out or cruelly drowned. It is a medical fact that drowning an animal of any age, even it is only a few hours old, is cruel, causing great pain. The only humane way to kill an animal is by an injection, which only a veterinary surgeon or animal clinic or doctor can arrange.

So you see, it is *not* cruel to prevent your cat from having unwanted kittens. But it *is* cruel to let him or her bring kittens indiscriminately into the world. You should think very seriously about the future when you take on the responsibility of looking after a cat or kitten. It isn't good enough if you look at coloured photographs of cats and say 'Oh, aren't they beautiful?' but fail to care for the future of your own cat at home. Kittens are lovable and attractive to look at, but it is a crime against nature to allow them to come into the world unless you can be sure they will be properly cared for and given every chance of enjoying a full, happy life.

These kittens — unlike many — have a good home and can look forward to the future. A good home is, among other things, a milk bowl and a place to scamper. Please note that each should have his *own* bowl — even though he may prefer his neighbour's

Buying a Kitten

Don't get the idea that cats are mainly for old ladies. It isn't true. They make ideal pets for young people and they can be left happily at home when you're out on a date or at the movies or a party, because they are extraordinarily self-sufficient. It isn't even correct to think that cats attach themselves to places and houses rather than people. They usually claim one master or mistress, especially the owner of the hand that feeds and strokes them, and even when they are kittens they soon get to know who owns them — or the person whom *they* own.

People are usually attracted by kittens, but it must be remembered that kittens soon grow up. So if you want a kitten, or are lucky enough to be given one, you must look ahead to the day when it will be quite a big cat and you must be prepared to care for him not only when he is a small bundle of fur but also when he is large and growing much older.

In Britain three main types of domestic cat are recognized — British, Manx and Foreign. Although there are many breeds of cats the majority of them in Britain, Europe and the United States vary only in colour or the length and quality of their coats. Most household cats are of the 'British' variety, with short bodies, broad round heads, small ears and short thick tails. The Manx is distinctive because he has no tail and his hind legs are longer than his forelegs. In the 'Foreign' type the body is long and slender, the legs are longer, and the head is narrow and tends to be wedge-shaped instead of round, while the tail is long and tapering. Perhaps the best example of this type is the popular Siamese, among the most intelligent of household pets, a companion of strong character with loyalty and good-humour among his many virtues.

Cats are very strong-willed and, you will not be able to make your pet do anything he doesn't wish. You can whistle to a dog and he will come running, but a cat will take no notice unless he wishes to, and then only if he knows and trusts you. A cat may be trained, but only as far as he

This is Tina. She is no bigger than the palm of your hand

32

desires. It is therefore best to start training him when he is a kitten, curious and willing to learn. But you had better realize straightaway that it is almost impossible to stop a cat climbing on to chairs, tables and beds.

Suppose you wish to choose a kitten instead of having one given to you. Well, think about it carefully before you decide. Remember that there are at least six million cats in Britain alone, about 50 million in the United States, many millions more in other countries, and that too many of them are neglected and unwanted. First you must make sure you are the right kind of person to own a cat. Will you have time to spare for him? Will you feed him regularly, nurse him when ill, and care for him properly? If not, forget about cats and buy a new record player; it needs less attention. But once you've said *yes* there are certain simple rules to be observed.

First, the kitten or cat you choose must be fit and healthy, active and sturdy, with a good coat and bright eyes. Kittens from pet shops are likely to have cat fleas (which won't show if the coat is dark) but they can soon be dusted free. Never use a powder containing D.D.T., which is poisonous to cats. Buy a powder from your chemist or pet shop or animal clinic. Your veterinary surgeon or local clinic should also check him for worms, mites in the ears, and other disorders.

Second, a pedigree cat from a good cattery is more likely to be free from disease or disorders than a kitten picked up in a back-street pet shop or a lost cats' home. But in spite of this, there is no reason why your perfect companion shouldn't be found in a strays' home, or at a pet dealer's, and be just as intelligent and even more attractive than the champion of champions. Whatever breed you chose, Siamese or Birman or Manx or Blue Persian or simple household tabby or ginger-coloured farmhouse mouser, it is wise to have him examined by a veterinary surgeon, if possible *before* you buy the cat, but if not possible — very soon afterwards.

You may feel inclined, once you have taken the kitten home, to treat it rather like a doll or new toy and to keep lifting it up. Remember that a kitten tires quickly and that all cats need a great deal of sleep. Don't let children pull a kitten around. He's much weaker than they are.

The wise cat owner is the one who has prepared a home for his new

Will you feed us, nurse us and care for us, even when we grow up?

pet before bringing him back. A personal basket with a clean, often-changed blanket or pillow should be placed away from draughts in a corner and it should be kept in the same place. Clean the basket out regularly and shake the blanket out of doors. Cats hate draughts, which can give them colds.

Long before you take the kitten home you should become acquainted with some information about feeding. When kittens are born they are deaf and blind and their eyes do not open until the ninth or tenth day. When six or seven weeks old, they should be gradually weaned away from their mother and should be encouraged to drink and eat from bowls. During their sixth or seventh week they can be taught to lap milk and will soon enjoy it. The milk can be introduced to them at the bowl by dipping your finger in the liquid and wetting the kittens' mouths. Cows' milk has little nourishment value for cats; goats' milk or condensed milk (slightly diluted with water) is better. Soon the youngsters will learn to eat small meals of finely chopped meat, a little boiled fish chopped up, some scraped raw meat, or cereals. The size of the meals should be increased gradually until at about six months the kittens will be enjoying adult feeding. Three or four small meals a day will be necessary after the ninth week, and during weeks 6-9 a little halibut oil should be added to the milk to help teeth and bones to grow stronger.

If you are buying a kitten he should be not less than ten or eleven weeks old. It really doesn't matter if he is older, but it is nice to see a kitten grow up and to train him. No kitten should be taken away from his mother until he is over eight weeks old.

One of the best ways of determining what the new arrival is going to eat is to ask his previous owner what he has been used to. Some cats like fish, others won't touch it. Not all cats like milk. Remember that a cat has a small stomach and that kittens are naturally greedy, so don't overdo the helpings. A balanced diet should include raw or cooked meat, rabbit or poultry if it has been carefully boned, liver as an occasional substitute because it is rich in vitamins, cooked fish (never raw) from which all bones have been removed, and vegetables if they are acceptable. Like humans, different cats have personal likes and dislikes about food. Cereals are often

Seek expert advice from a veterinary surgeon

Kittens need plenty of sleep, away from draughts

acceptable, and yeast (which can be bought in tablet form specially made up for animals) is valuable.

Not all cats like milk; many prefer water, and a bowl of fresh water should always be handy, just as his own food bowl must be near at hand, preferably being put down in the same place for each meal. Bowls should be washed after use or they will collect dirt and flies.

Some people rely on tinned foods for their cats but it is doubtful if even the best-known and most frequently advertised brands contain all the nourishment which is needed. Certainly, no wise cat owner will feed his pet exclusively on tinned food, but an occasional tin will do little harm. It can be no substitute, however, for a varied diet based on fresh meat or fish or rabbit or game.

You will find that a kitten is naturally clean. His mother may already have trained him in toilet matters, but if not he can soon be taught. If you have a garden or yard take him out and place him on the earth. Now, very gently, draw his two front paws over the soil with a scratching action. He will know instinctively what you mean, because cats use their front paws to cover up the place where they have squatted. If you live in a flat or house with no garden the kitten will need a sanitary tray lined with dry earth or newspaper, and this must be cleaned out regularly.

Whatever breed you choose, even if like most cats he is no known breed, he will require daily grooming, his coat brushing and combing, so that all loose hairs are removed. If they are not removed the cat will swallow hairs when he licks his coat to clean himself and they will form a ball in his stomach which he will try to bring up by coughing and being sick. Sometimes it is difficult, and occasionally impossible, for the furball or hairball to come up, or to be passed through the body. In this case it will be necessary to call in the vet. But there is one way of ensuring that your cat *does* bring up furballs and that is by encouraging him to eat grass. It contains vitamins, aids the digestion, and wraps itself around the hair in the stomach so that it all comes up together. Cocksfoot grass is the best kind, but you will find that your cat will eat most types of grass if you give him the chance.

To stop the kitten scratching at the furniture you should provide a scratch-

A healthy kitten is active and sturdy, with a good coat and bright eyes

ing post or piece of wood. On this he will appear to be sharpening his claws, but he is really attempting to clean them and to stop them growing too long. There is no reason why he shouldn't be taught to keep those dangerous claws sheathed when he is picked up or is near you. A firm but gentle rebuke and a gentle tap on the paws will soon teach him. It is much more unlikely that you will ever be able to train him not to chase and catch birds, or to steal food if you leave it around on plates in the kitchen. Cats have little sense of what you think is right or wrong, but they have been successfully taught not to attack chickens and other creatures, and cats on farms soon learn how to behave.

If you already have a cat in the house when your new young friend arrives you may find that the present owner is jealous. Cats seem to feel that they *own* the homes in which they live and they don't always accept intruders. A kitten, however, is usually accepted if the introduction is carefully handled. The solution is to give the older inhabitant a little more attention than he usually gets, together with some extra food, all in full view of the new arrival. Thus, he should associate the kitten with a new lease of life.

Cats must be inoculated against feline enteritis, and this should be done when they are nine or ten weeks old. Feline infectious enteritis is the oldest of all cat diseases, and for kittens under fifteen months old it is the most deadly and infectious. It was known in central Europe as long ago as the fifth century and it is still highly fatal unless proper precautions are taken *before* the cat is infected. Cats in a colony or neighbourhood are often infected together, dying off as if they were all poisoned. In most countries the hottest months are the most dangerous.

The first signs of the illness come suddenly. First the temperature rises to about 103 degrees. But you will not notice this. Your first indication that all is not well will be a general listlessness and apathy. You will be surprised to see the cat sitting over his bowl of water or food, which he refuses or seems unable to touch. It is as if the bowl fascinates him, yet he will not stoop to eat or drink. At this stage he is probably in pain and if you have not already called in the vet, do so at once. If you are unable to summon a vet you may have to take the

Where's my mum?

patient to an animal clinic. In that case wrap him up well in a warm blanket. But do remember that if he has enteritis — or even the more modest cat 'flu — you may easily infect other cats by taking him to a clinic.

The second stage comes soon after, when he is sick, bringing up a brown or green frothy mucus, to his great distress, because cats are naturally clean and they hate making a mess. If he is picked up he will utter a faint cry. With a kitten, you are probably now too late to save him. Death follows quickly, not more than twenty per cent of young cats being able to recover. Your vet will probably agree that at this stage it is kinder to put the patient to sleep. But those who do manage to get over the disaster are likely to be immune for life.

To see this scourge spreading through a family of kittens is a heartbreaking experience. I have explained in detail what happens because it is important to realize what *might* occur with any kitten if precautions are not taken very soon after he has left his mother. Fortunately, the solution is simple. There is now a vaccine made from harmless emulsion which will protect the young cat from being unexpectedly overwhelmed by this terrible disease. Two injections for a nine week old kitten are better than one. It is not difficult. Consult your vet or local animal clinic. It will be too late if the disease strikes. Also, you must remember that any grown cat can bring the infection indoors on his paws or fur, having picked up the virus from another cat. It spreads quickly around a district, it can be carried on boots or shoes or clothes or on your hands, and pet shops are often full of it. Even you, handling a kitten which is suffering from it, can pass it on when you pick up another cat. When you call in the vet, ask him about disinfecting yourself and the house. The animal's bedding and basket should be burnt. No other cats should be brought into the house for at least six months.

If you don't want or can't afford to pay a vet to examine or treat your cat you should, in all cases of emergency (and at least once a year for a routine check-up), go instead to one of the several animal clinics, such as the Blue Cross, Royal Society for the Prevention of Cruelty to Animals, P.D.S.A, or Cats' Protection League.

There's a very big world beyond the window-sill

Did someone say cream cakes for tea?

Excuse us if we stare, but everything's a bit new to us

A Dozen Don'ts

1. DON'T take a kitten under eight weeks old away from its mother.

2. DON'T give him a monotonous diet of tinned food or fish every day. Vary his food, and ensure that he has milk or water each day in a clean bowl.

3. DON'T neglect his coat. He needs brushing and combing regularly.

4. DON'T give him a leather collar, it might get caught up in branches. If you must give him a collar, choose an expanding one.

5. DON'T go on holiday and leave him uncared for, he can't fend for himself and he will need daily food and attention.

6. DON'T let children maul him around when he is a kitten. He is weak, very sensitive, and may be frightened. He gets tired easily, and needs plenty of sleep.

7. DON'T regard your cat, however attractive he is, as the only one in the world. It is not wrong to spoil him — cats need love and attention, which they amply repay — but the person who genuinely loves animals will respect *all* dumb creatures, not only the one sitting at home in front of the fire.

8. DON'T ever hit a cat, or any other animal. If you talk sensibly and firmly to your pet he will understand. But remember that cats are more independent than most animals, so it won't do any good if you lose your temper. You have to gain the confidence of a cat, and this can only be done if you really care for him. Cats are extraordinary, the way they can judge humans.

Don't leave him alone for very long

Do brush and comb his coat regularly

9. DON'T leave your cat out at night or let him wander around dustbins. That is where disease and trouble lie.

10. DON'T get rid of unwanted pets to dealers or pet shops unless you are certain that they won't be sold to vivisection laboratories or hospitals. If your local animal welfare society cannot find a home for unwanted kittens, ask your vet or animal clinic to put them painlessly to sleep. Whatever you do, DON'T try to do it yourself, it is a job for an animal doctor, an expert.

11. DON'T introduce a new kitten into a house where there are already other cats or a dog without first making sure that he will be accepted, and won't be terrified.

12. DON'T forget that Ginger or Snowy or Charlie is a member of the household who will be a devoted member of the family if you care for him and give him the affection which all need, humans and animals alike.

Cats also need a certain amount of sunny solitude

Sensitivity

A cat's ears are very sensitive and are used as an aid to hunting birds and mice. Watch how he turns his ears to pick up sounds. His whiskers are also extremely sensitive and are used as instruments of touch. There is an old saying that if a cat with long whiskers puts his head through a hole, then he can squeeze his body through. Whiskers help a cat to move around in the dark, and cats living in cellars grow longer whiskers than those reared in daylight.

A cat's sense of smell is particularly sensitive. Carl van Vechten, writing in his book *The Tiger in the House*, has told how during the first world war the British government conscripted five hundred thousand cats, some of which were sent to sea to test the air in submarines while the remainder went to the trenches where their warnings of the approach of poison gas, apparent long before any soldier could smell it, saved many lives.

Your cat may not have a chance to be so heroic, but he will sense the presence of a stranger in your house, his home, before he has even seen him.

Long whiskers are extremely sensitive as instruments of touch

Their greatest use is as an aid to moving around in the dark

Cats are easily startled by noise and movement

General alert! Isn't that a bird?

Keeping Fit

Cats do not need as much exercise as dogs, but they like freedom to move around from room to room and it is best — unless you live in a flat or on a main road — to allow your pet free access to and from the house. The problem of opening and closing doors can be solved by having a magnetic cat door built into the back door. They are draught-proof, and it is unlikely that a stray cat will know how to use one.

Some Siamese and Abyssinians like being taken out on a collar and lead, and many cats will follow their owners along pavements and into shops. But there is no need to regulate a cat's exercise. Give him an open door, or a cat door, and he will go in and out without disturbing you. Don't turn him out at night to fend for himself, for cats feel the cold. On the other hand, never shut him indoors for hours on end. Just give him enough room to 'swing a cat' and he'll devise his own swinging exercises.

Cats can leap great distances, and they never miss their target

Mrs Crump had indignantly assured him that there wasn't room to swing a cat there; but as Mr Dick justly observed to me, sitting down on the foot of the bed, nursing his leg, 'You know, Trotwood, I don't want to swing a cat. I never do swing a cat. Therefore, what does that signify to me?'

From *David Copperfield* by Charles Dickens

The alley cat above is trying to emulate his larger cousin, the cheetah

Don't worry, a cat always lands on its feet

Cuddles (below) wants to be a ballet dancer when he grows up

Exercise comes naturally whether he is playing with a ball of paper or simply completing his toilet

Curiosity

Curiosity is said to have killed the cat, but did it? Cats are fascinated by moving objects, and kittens are especially curious. Watch a youngster playing with his mother's tail, or with his own, or give a table-tennis ball or a piece of screwed-up paper to play with and he will never stop playing. This will not stop him climbing up the curtains, clambering onto the table, or scratching at the backs of armchairs, but it will keep him happy and will build up his muscles.

Apart from cotton reels and rubber mice, the best plaything for a kitten is another kitten. A small kitten without mother or companions is a lonely sight, but when you see kittens tumbling over one another at play, or scrambling for their food, you can't help wishing that they would never grow up.

Open a carrier bag next to a cat and he will eye it with great curiosity, and will then probably get inside and sit down. Why? Simply because a paper bag is warm and draught-proof. An equally comfortable nest may be a drawer, a clothes cupboard, or a shelf among some very dry books. It isn't always curiosity, it is often sheer intelligence.

Crawling under the furniture ... curiosity or sheer intelligence?

A tangle of ticker-tape and two curious cats

Look, I'm a catrobat   Now watch this   Got it!

I wonder if there's something here for me.   I'll have to take a closer look

Up we go

Help, I'm slipping!

Catastrophe!

None of these will do

Guess what! I'm a catalogue!

What's this, a flying fish?

Just a paw's length away from trouble

You should have seen the one that got away

Siamese

The Siamese is one of the most popular of breeds, not quite like any other, but among the most affectionate, loyal and intelligent of cats. They like human company even more than other breeds and they will follow you around, go out walking on a lead, and become extremely talkative, with a wide variety of expressive voice ranges. They have a distinctive, harsh, strange voice which sometimes sounds like a human cry.

Medium in size, they have long, slim bodies with long tapering tails. The head is long, the eyes are wide and slanting and oriental, the ears are large and pricked up, and the colour of the coat is usually pale fawn with a cream chest and stomach. The colour of the coat grows darker with age, and the mask, which is a feature of the breed, is not complete until the kitten is almost fully grown.

There are four recognized varieties. The Siamese Seal-Point is marked brown on his face, ears, feet and tail. The Blue-Pointed Siamese has blue marks instead of brown, a fine close coat, bright blue eyes, and a white body shading into blue. The Chocolate-Pointed Siamese is ivory coloured, shading to a rich milk chocolate, and also has bright blue eyes. The fourth variety is the Lilac-Pointed Siamese, which has a white coat, a nose tipped with mauve, blue eyes, and lilac toes and pads.

Usually devoted to only one of the family, the Siamese will run to greet his master or mistress, purring loudly. If you are lucky enough to own one, you will understand why it is said that the first Siamese was born in Noah's Ark, his father being a monkey and his mother a tiger. Most cats are thieves by nature, especially if the larder door is left open, but Siamese are really professional at silently nipping in and stealing the joint or a steak directly your back is turned.

The classic Siamese is short-haired (above), but experimental breeding has produced the long-haired variety shown below

Friendship

To gain the friendship of a cat is a difficult thing. The cat is a philosophical, methodical, quiet animal, tenacious of his own habits, fond of order and cleanliness, and does not lightly confer his friendship. If you are worthy of his affection, a cat will be your friend but never your slave. He keeps his free will though he loves, and will not do for you what he thinks unreasonable; but if he once gives himself to you, it is with absolute confidence and fidelity of affection. He makes himself the companion of your hours of solitude, melancholy and toil. He will remain for whole evenings on your knee, uttering a contented purr, happy to be with you. Put him down and he will jump up again with a sort of cooing sound like a gentle reproach; and sometimes he will sit upon the carpet in front of you looking at you with eyes so melting, so caressing and so human, that they almost frighten you, for it is impossible to believe that a soul is not there.

Théophile Gautier

'He makes himself the companion of your hours of solitude'

A friend that fits in the crook of your arm

Cats' Eyes

The ancient Egiptians believed that the changes in the eyes of cats were governed by the movements of the sun and moon. We know that a cat's eyes can expand widely with pure innocence or surprise and can also contract to mere slits. Of course, it really all depends on the brightness of the light. The old belief that cats see in the dark is false, but it is very nearly true. They can see in poor light and their sharp eyes respond to the smallest glimmer or beam. Watch Ginger as he sits up at the window and observe how he focuses on a pigeon sitting on a faraway roof or chimney top. It will take you twice as long to discover what has attracted his attention. But he noticed it at once.

Humans have only two eyelids but cats have three, the third being known as the haw. If the haws are visible it is likely that the cat is unwell or may soon be ill. Normally, you should not see that third eyelid.

A kitten's eyes will not start to open until ten or twelve days after birth. It is unlikely that they will remain closed after that time, but when they open — or if they don't — there may be a stickiness attached to the eyelids which can be bathed away if you dip a small piece of cotton wool into warm water and boracic and then very gently wash over the eyelids. The eyes should always be delicately washed. Adult cats often collect dirt and stains around the eyes, and these should be cleared away, or infection may follow.

NEVER take a kitten out into the sun to be photographed or admired. He must be at least five or six weeks old before he goes out of doors. Until then the best place for him is the dark or the shaded place or basket or cupboard or box in which he was born. In his own good time he will discover the room, then the house, and finally the great outside world. Don't rush him, let him find out about it gradually.

Ointment is not advisable for a cat's eyes unless it has been prescribed by a veterinary surgeon. A little Vaseline may be gently applied after bathing, to ease any inflammation or swelling. But do take care, those beautiful eyes are precious.

A ginger cat with eyes to match his coat

I spy with my little eye

Large expressive green eyes are a characteristic of the Chinchilla breed

Cat Shows

The first official cat show in Britain took place at London's Crystal Palace in 1871 and six years later the National Cat Club was founded. For the first time, a register of pedigree cats was kept and the standards of breeds were fixed. In 1909 the Governing Council of the Cat Fancy emerged, to which most of Britain's and many overseas clubs are affiliated. Because of this Council's work, and the efforts of similar organizations abroad, pedigree cats are now greatly in demand. What is more, the whole status of the cat as a pet and companion has been raised. In the United States, similar work is carried out by the American Cat Association, the Cat Fanciers' Association, and the Cat Fanciers' Federation. The first Australian show was in 1925. Five years later New Zealand's Governing Council was formed. Canadian cat shows are run on American lines. In every country the pedigree cat has helped to make your cat and mine more respectable, acceptable, and better cared for.

In Britain most shows take place between September and February inclusive, except for kitten shows, which are held in summer. The largest English show is run by the National Cat Club each December at Olympia, London. Most of the big shows are organized by the clubs, such as the Siamese Cat Club, the Burmese Cat Club, the Brown Tabby Society, the Black and White Cat Club, the Russian Blue Cat Club, and many others. These clubs are always ready to give advice and help beginners. Many districts and towns also organize shows. But they are seldom well-advertised before the event. In Britain you can obtain a list of shows from the Secretary of the Governing Council of the Cat Fancy, Mrs S. Berliner, 146 Western Avenue, East Acton, London, W. 3, if you will send her a stamped, addressed envelope and 6d. for a list. For details about show procedure you should seek the advice of the Hon. Secretary of the Feline Advisory Bureau, The Barn Cottage, Tytherington, Falfield, Gloucestershire. This organization does splendid work for cats' welfare.

Before deciding to show your cat you should visit at least one show, to

This Siamese Blue-point was a winner at the Paris International Cat Show

Blue-cream kitten at the National Cat Club Championship Show in London

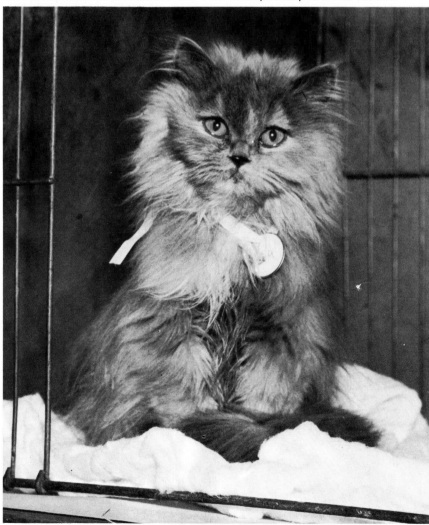

see what happens. If you look at the entries you can determine what chance your pet has. You will observe that the prize-winners are all well-groomed and in perfect condition.

Besides their good-grooming, however, each cat must have the recognized characteristics of his particular breed. For instance, a cat entered in the 'Black' class must have an absolutely jet black coat. Each hair must be completely black from root to tip. Similarly a 'White' cat must be completely white with not one hair of any other colour. Tabbies have as rigid qualifications as any other breed. A striped tabby must be gray with vertical black stripes along its sides and a single black stripe running down the centre of the back from head to tip of tail. There is an M-shaped black marking on the forehead, two horizontal black lines on the cheek and black bands called 'bracelets' on the legs. Brown Tabbies and Silver Tabbies are respectively brown and silver with still different markings.

The colour of a show cat's eyes are as important as the colour and markings of its coat. A Black must have orange eyes without a trace of green, and a White must have either blue or orange eyes. Siamese eyes must be blue, and in a silver Tabby blue-green eyes are preferred.

The standards by which a cat is judged include several other categories besides colour of coat and eyes. Some things that matter are the condition of the coat, the proportions of the body, the shape of the head, the shape of the eyes, and in some breeds the length and condition of the tail. For each of these categories a certain number of points may be gained, the total possible points adding up to 100.

If you want to check your cat's characteristics against those of the show cats, see *The Observer's Book of Cats* by Grace Pond in which all recognized breeds are described. This book is also helpful if you are seriously considering entering your cat in a show.

But even if — like most cats — yours is obviously not a potential champion, you can still enter him. Long-haired cats belonging to no recognized breed may be entered under 'Any Other Colour' and short-haired cats may be entered under 'Any Other Variety'. At many shows there are prizes for non-registered household pets, novices, juniors, etc. and sometimes for 'the most friendly

Candyboy of Dunesk, a Cream kitten, waits to be judged at a London show

Charlie, a tabby of uncertain origin, won the 'Pet of the Year' trophy

cat' or 'the prettiest cat in the show'.

Show rules vary slightly in different countries, and it is wise to make yourself thoroughly acquainted with the procedure and regulations before going to the hall.

All cats entered in *any* show must be immunized against feline infectious enteritis, and no unhealthy cat should be taken to a show.

Don't expect your cat to take kindly to being penned up in his cage for the first time. He should be introduced to a pen long before he goes to the show. It is a small place in which to house an animal all day.

At the end of the show (although you are not allowed to talk to judges before or during the judging) you are able to discuss with them and with other owners the various points which have led to success or failure. It is at these Championship Shows that breeders and cat owners exchange ideas and learn about the latest developments in the cat world. Here, where all the most perfect cats seem to be gathered together in one hall, you can see the beautiful Chinchillas, the rare Birmans, the Russian Blues, the White Persians, the Blue-pointed Siamese, and you can meet their owners and ask questions. Cat owners, like their pets, are usually friendly, and are only too pleased to do what we all like doing — talk about cats.

This is not the place for a full description of the procedure which must be strictly observed when showing a cat. You will see what happens when you visit your first show as a spectator. But don't consider entering a cat which is highly nervous or likely to become upset. Then, when you are satisfied that you understand the routine, have a go. There are usually challenge certificates, silver cups, rosettes and money prizes to be won, and sometimes special awards like cat baskets, blankets, and chocolates. But even if Ginger doesn't win anything, don't be disappointed. You can learn a great deal about looking after cats, whether you go to a show as an exhibitor or a spectator.

Two pampered Siamese Seal-points, aged 4½ months

Two impatient Abyssinians, aged 11 weeks

Am I the prettiest cat in the show?

'Well, then' the Cat went on, 'you see a dog growls when it's angry, and wags its tail when it's pleased. Now *I* growl when I'm pleased, and wag my tail when I'm angry. Therefore I'm mad.'

'*I* call it purring, not growling,' said Alice.

'Call it what you like,' said the Cat. 'Do you play croquet with the Queen today?'

Mad Cats

The Cheshire Cat was not the only cat to cultivate enigmatic expressions. In fact, the famous feline 'inscrutability' is probably due to the ambiguity of cats' facial expressions as much as anything else. The most usual aspect is a rather placid one of watchful content. But when a cat pulls a face who can honestly tell whether it is an expression of gaiety or woe?

Show cats seem to be especially good at putting their best face forward. But the three pictured on this page and the page following have also cultivated the art of mad inscrutability. Tania, top right, is a blue Persian, chosen the 'champion of champions' at a Paris show. She isn't exactly dancing around her cage in delight, but then perhaps she always looks as if she were pouting. Below right, a long-haired Cream Persian glowers — or grins — at the judges of the National Cat Club's Championship Show in London. Is he self-satisfied or furious?

Undoubtedly the madcat prize goes to a Siamese kitten named Supra Echo, pictured on the following page. Is this an example of high animal spirits or extreme displeasure? Glad, sad or just plain mad?

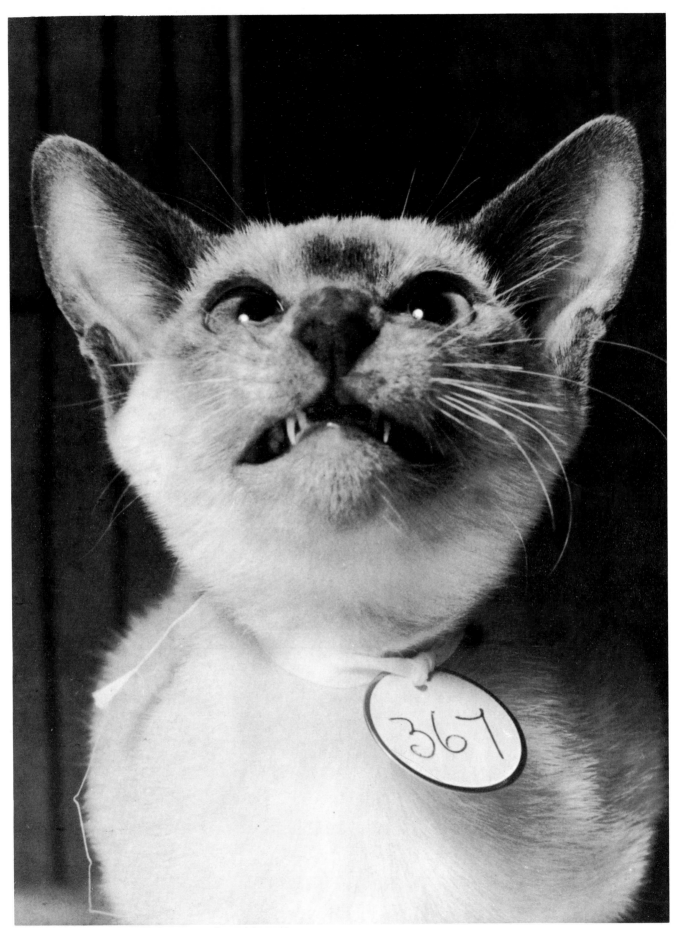

I wish the judges would hurry up. I want to go home

Doors

Cats are as indipendent in their comings and goings as they are in every other aspect of life. They go out when they want to go out. They come in when they want to come in. They do not have to be taken out, like dogs. But unless they're very clever, they do have to wait for someone to open the door. To remedy this situation, in which feline pride so obviously suffers, Paul Gallico passes on the following advice — straight from the cat's mouth:

Doors are a problem in any house you will ever live in, and you simply have to learn to cope with them, or rather, with your people, and teach them the necessity of dropping whatever they happen to be doing to open one of them to let you in or out.

If you are fortunate you will have taken over a family both sufficiently cat-minded as well as ingenious to rig up one of those patent affairs cut into the bottom of the front door, which enables us to come and go as we please.

This, of course, is ideal for everyone, particularly for us, and enables us to get out at night without a lot of questions and admonitions. However, this does not solve the problem of inside doors, the ones to rooms, closets, cupboards, cellars, attics etc. and the rule that you must try to establish at your earliest possible opportunity is that they must be *left open at all times.* You may have some difficulty with those leading from one room to another, or connecting with hallways, since the male of the family will be shouting about draughts, but there is no reason whatsoever why closet or cupboard doors should be kept shut.

You can learn very quickly how to open a door yourself, particularly if it is of the bent-handle kind, which you can work merely by getting up on your hind legs and putting your weight upon it. The round, doorknob handle is somewhat more of a problem, but when you have your full growth and weight you will find that by pushing or pulling on it you can get it to turn sufficiently to slip the latch.

However, when you have learned these tricks, don't — under any cir-

This cat flap shows the principle of the cat door. The best cat doors are made of stronger stuff, and many are magnetic

cumstances — let your family know that you have. It is their business and absolute concern to open and shut doors for you at any time, and your own little skill you will keep to yourself for use at such times as when you may suddenly find yourself shut in a cupboard or when, for some reason or other, you are forbidden to go out.

To come in from the outside, scratching on the door and a good, loud miaow will alert someone. For an inside job, if your people are properly conditioned, it will be necessary to do no more than to go and sit by the door and just look at it. If that doesn't work pretty soon, you turn and look at them. If they are busy doing something give your miaow that they have come to connect with impatience. Whichever, remember that once you have attracted their attention to the fact that you want to get out, never let them go back to what they were doing. In any well-regulated household you come first.

From *The Silent Miaow* by Paul Gallico

This kind of door is a cinch to open

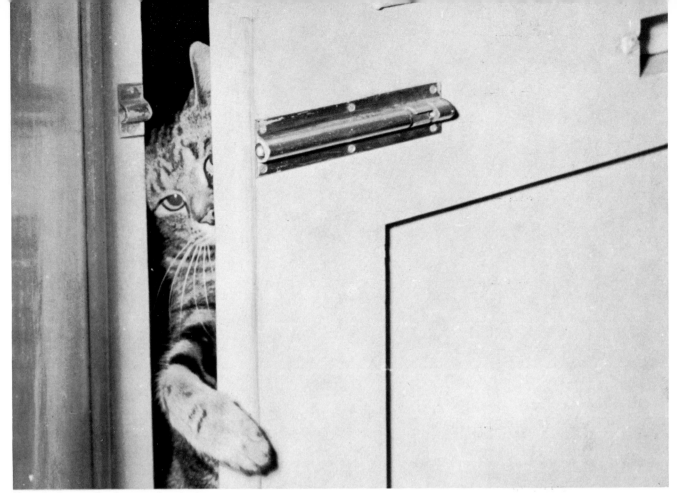

Now, just a gentle shove and we're in

But this sort of lock presents a real problem

A Pinta, Please

Cats are generally believed to be slaves to the milk bowl, and a kitten will soon learn to lap it all up, but it must be remembered that cow's milk is about 90 per cent water and is no substitute for good food. The other ten per cent is made up of fat, sugar, albumin and casein, and has nourishment value. Milk is no substitute for an adequate supply of fresh water provided in a clean bowl every day. Furthermore, too much milk often causes diarrhoea. Goat's milk or tinned milk is better than bottled cow's milk, and even this is not so valuable as a mother cat's milk. In places where cow's milk is pasteurized it is advisable to add a few drops of halibut liver oil to your kitten's food, to prevent rickets. An extra pint of Milka may suit humans, but it doesn't provide the balanced diet that a cat requires, no matter how readily a kitten may rush to the bowl. Kittens are always greedy, and they can't be expected to know what is best for them.

I'm sure no one will mind if I help myself

Getting down to some serious drinking from a cask full of milk

They'll never miss this one.

Some cats like to drink from a clean saucer.

Others aren't so fussy

It tastes better if you get it all over your face

I wish I had a longer tongue

Home, Sweet Home

Cats love home life and hate being moved to a new house or flat. If you move to another neighbourhood you will find that your friend is not so keen on moving as you are, even if you're going up in the world. It is advisable to move all the furniture first and then to take your cat along personally, last of all, in a basket or box with air holes. Cats have been known to sit for days outside an empty house, wondering what has happened to upset the life they have come to accept. When he arrives in his new home he may be suspicious because he won't recognize the rooms or the lay-out of the furniture. You will need to talk to him, to reassure him, and to make a fuss of him until he settles down. An old-fashioned theory, which often works, says that if you put butter on his paws he will be so busy licking it off that he won't have time to think about going out in search of his old home and familiar surroundings. If he has been used to stairs, he may be surprised to find none in your smart new flat. It is wise not to let him out of doors until he has become accustomed to the new lay-out. Just in case he dashes back to the old house — and cats have been known to travel many miles — it is advisable to arrange with a neighbour close to your old home to telephone or get in touch with you if your cat returns there.

Warmth, comfort and a little extra petting should soon persuade him to settle down. What's a home without your favourite cat sitting in front of the fire or curled up by your feet? Puss may choose strange places in which to settle down. But it is really *you*, the master who feeds him and cares for him, whom he prefers. Home is where the master is.

Wood Green Animal Shelter at Heydon, Hertfordshire

A barnyard makes a perfect home

For the Spanish cat, home is where he takes his siesta

Some make a home where they find it

Others are pampered from birth

Having a Family

Unlike the female dog, the female cat (or queen) is usually irregular in her mating 'seasons' and the problem which faces owners is more serious because the time to board her out or restrain her from wandering is never known.

The queen usually comes in heat about three times a year, for a period of from three days to three weeks. During this period she usually 'calls' for a mate, making an almost child-like cry or caterwauling, which can sound very eerie at night. At this time she may appear more than usually affectionate, and will probably roll about on the carpet, purring loudly.

The natural instinct is for the queen to go roaming out of doors, and it will be difficult to restrain her, especially if your family forgets to shut doors. If she is in this condition the male cat will always find her, lying in wait during her limited exercise periods.

The male leaves a strong, unpleasant smell which brings out in the queen the desire to be mated. When this is her desire she forgets about humans, home and food. Stud or arranged mating is quite different from natural or wild mating. In such cases the queen is usually sent to the tom, and they are introduced slowly, meeting first in separate compartments. When they start crooning or singing together they are ready to meet.

At her first mating the queen may resent her partner's intrusion and will probably scratch and claw. When mating is completed the tom quickly leaps away and the queen sits down to wash herself.

The normal period of pregnancy, or gestation as it is called, is from 55 to 65 days. The kittens should have been born by the 69th day. If it is the first time your cat is having a litter you should take her to the veterinary surgeon or animal clinic as soon as you realize she is going to have a family. However, most cats have little difficulty in bearing their offspring without human aid.

The mother will usually choose the place where the family is to be born, but it is wise to prepare a nest for her about ten days before the day.

Future parents

Choose a bed for her in a dark, sheltered, warm place away from draughts and sunlight. Introduce her to the bed and take her there several times, but don't be surprised if at the last moment she selects a totally different place of her own. She may scratch around in cupboards or a chest of drawers and will probably tear up newspapers to form a nest, paper being warm and comfortable. When she does this you may be sure that the day is not far off. Torn-up paper makes an excellent temporary cover for a blanket, since it can be destroyed easily when the kittens have been born.

She will probably not wish to eat until she has had the kittens, and she may become restless. Don't fuss over her and don't get worried. Cats have been giving birth to kittens by the score for millions of years and they know instinctively what to do. When she retires to her nest, leave her alone for a while and then go quietly and have a look at her.

There are usually four to eight kittens in a litter, but Siamese cats often have larger families. Each tiny animal is born in a sac which breaks open at birth, or is bitten open by the mother, who also severs the umbilical cord which connects her to the kitten, and swallows the after-birth. It is very unlikely that she will fail to break the cord but if she hesitates you may have to sever the cord yourself with a pair of *blunt* rather than sharp scissors. The mother gnaws at the cord to sever it, and does not break it sharply.

The kittens will be born at intervals of about half-an-hour. The mother will wash each kitten as it arrives, and you will not know how many there are to come until they have all arrived. Don't clean up the paper until next day. Leave her alone with the kittens and don't fuss her. Give her a bowl of warm condensed milk diluted with a little water. She will not leave the babies, so you must put a litter tray just outside the nest, and keep it clean. Don't give her big meals during the first twenty-four hours, but then return her to her normal diet with some extra nourishing food such as rabbit or minced beef.

Unwanted kittens should be taken away immediately after birth and should be handed at once to a veterinary surgeon or animal clinic. Don't destroy them yourself, it is a job for

A family can be a nuisance when mother is trying to sleep

Bedtime for a tired kitten

an expert. Drowning at any stage is cruel and painful, even if the kitten has just been born. Unwanted kittens should be injected by a vet so that they fall asleep immediately and without pain.

The youngsters will not develop a sense of smell or taste until about the third day, but even soon after birth they will begin crawling around their mother looking for milk. They are born deaf and blind and will not open their eyes until about the seventh or eighth day. They should not be taken out into daylight during the first three weeks because their eyes are very weak. If there is stickiness around the eyelids wash them very gently with warm water and boracic and dry with cotton wool. At first the kittens will not move far from the nest but after about three weeks they will start staggering around, weakly at first, exploring the big world outside. Mind they don't get trodden on; don't let children pick them up and maul them around, they tire quickly.

After three weeks the kittens should be ready for weaning away from their mother's milk. Cows' milk has little nourishment value, so if you can get goats' milk or condensed milk, this will be more valuable. Add a few drops of halibut oil once a day. Soon the kittens will start to eat small meals and to roam around the house and chase their mother's tail.

A family of hedgehogs with their adopted mother

Mother keeps a watch because baby's eyes have only just opened

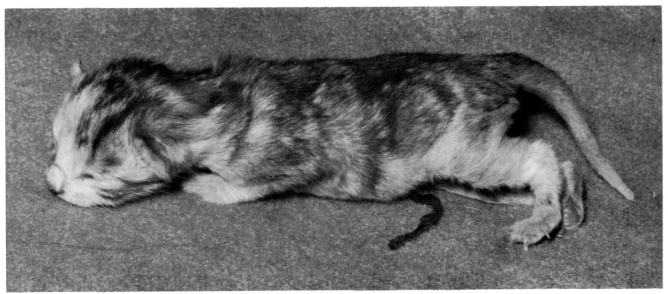

This newly-born tabby has already been washed by its mother

Please don't handle them until they're a little older!

Abyssinians

The Abyssinian was introduced to Britain from Abyssinia over a hundred years ago, but the breed — which was first shown at the Crystal Palace around 1883 — has since been greatly changed through breeding and development. The pedigree Abyssinian has a long face and is ruddy-brown ticked with black or dark markings. The head is long and pointed, the feet are small, the pads are black, the ears are sharp but broad at the base, and the large eyes are usually green, hazel, or yellow. A variation is the Red Abyssinian, which has a coat with a deeper red colour, but as with all Abyssinians the coat is short, fine and close.

When they are resting, Abyssinians look rather like young lions, but they are surprisingly playful, frisky and companionable, and they make delightful household pets.

Studying the dahlias

A Red Abyssinian

Waiting for Master

The old tradition that the faithful dog waits at the door and then runs and fetches his master's slippers and takes them to the fireside sounds nice, but it doesn't always happen. Rover often knocks you flying when he jumps up at you, and you have to shout 'Down boy, down!' and then disentangle him from your legs. Cats aren't quite so embarrassing and their affection is less obvious, but there is no doubt that they are delighted to see you come home, and frequently pine when you are away. Anyone who has gone on holiday for a few weeks and left Ginger in a cattery or with a neighbour knows this is true. Many cats wait by the door for their masters or mistresses to return, and when they hear the key go into the latch they start to purr.

The great French writer Alexandre Dumas wrote about his cat Mysouff. If he wasn't coming home to dinner that night the cat seemed to sense this, refusing to go out and lying motionless on his cushion 'like a serpent biting his own tail'. However, it was quite different on days when Dumas meant to return punctually. Then, if someone forgot to open the door for him, Mysouff would scratch at the door continuously until he got what he wanted and was let out. Quite contented, he would wander abroad, knowing that his master would return at the usual time.

I wonder why he hasn't come home?

Keeping his slippers warm

I'll keep an eye on the street

He's never been so late before

The Professionals

There are show cats who earn silver trophies and cheques for their owners, cats who simply sit at home in front of the fire and doze, cats who roam among the dustbins, and cats who never seem content unless they are bringing up families. But there is also another kind, which is too often forgotten. This is the working cat, the professional, the feline employed in a factory or restaurant or office or farm to catch mice and rats — in return for his keep.

There must be many thousands of them in warehouses and ships' holds and storerooms, guarding the world's food supplies, saving valuable merchandise, ensuring that bread and meat and sugar aren't nibbled away by hungry rodents. Cats have kept the dreaded Plague from spreading, they have in their time saved many a miller's store of corn, and ever since farming began they have fearlessly killed rats almost as big as themselves and sometimes twice as fierce.

Michael Joseph, the publisher and author who wrote two of the best cat books, *Charles* and *Cat's Company*, has told the story of Rufus, the large, sandy, official mouser of the British Treasury in London. One day in 1930 an important Treasury official noticed a mouse scampering down a corridor — with no Rufus in pursuit. Attention was immediately drawn to the meagre pay allotted to Rufus — a mere 2d a day — hardly enough to keep a mouse alive, much less a large cat. It was suggested that with the steadily increasing cost of living this was not enough. No wonder Rufus was working only part time. Shouldn't he be paid a living wage?

The Lords of the Treasury are said to have met and debated the matter but eventually decided (no doubt because of the National Debt or the Balance of Payments or some other excuse) that a pay increase of fifty per cent was too much. Things looked glum for Rufus, but fortunately Dame Maude Lawrence, then the head of the women in the civil service, privately enlisted the sympathy of the Chancellor of the Exchequer, who agreed that the Treasury cat should receive an extra penny a day.

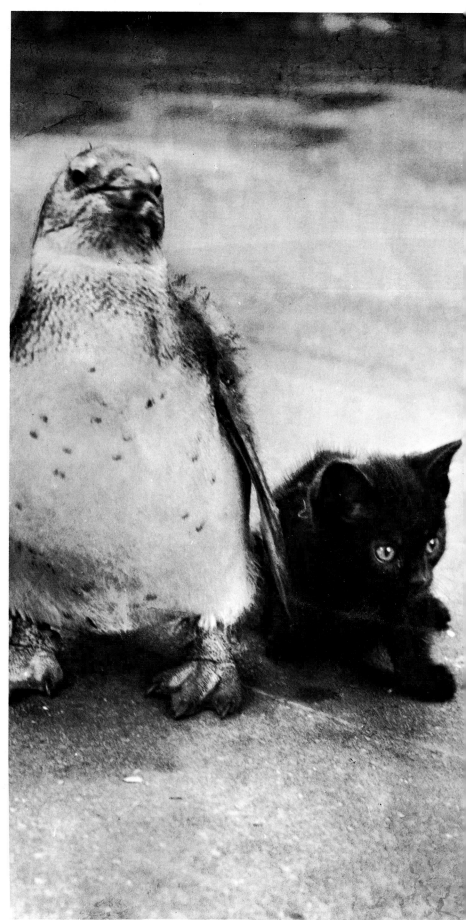

Peter the kitten and his penguin friend are employed at a children's zoo

Budgets for Polaris submarines and nuclear weapons and bombers are of course larger, and are usually settled more quickly. But Rufus got his extra pay, which meant more food, which in turn probably made him less inclined to catch mice. After all, who cares about chasing one's dinner if it is already presented on a plate?

In *Cat's Company* Mr Joseph tells the more remarkable story of Scissors, a black and white kitten which lived with him in the front line trenches during the 1914-18 war. Scissors used to follow his officer-master up the poppy-lined communication trenches and along the front line, and he was a great favourite with all the soldiers in the sector.

'Only a narrow strip of No-Man's Land separated us from the German front line. Scissors had a dangerous but playful habit of leaping gracefully onto the parapet and picking his way delicately along the broken ground, through the wire and over the massed sandbags, keeping pace with my orderly and myself as we made our cautious way below along the zig-zag of the front line. It must have been perfectly obvious to the enemy that Scissors was accompanying his officer on his morning round — indeed, one fine August morning we distinctly heard a laugh and a shout in guttural German from beyond the wire — but that part of the line was then known to both armies as 'peaceful' and no sniper or bomb-thrower tried his skill on the furry target.

'Scissors was wounded before we left the Arras sector by a stray fragment of shrapnel. It was, luckily, a flesh wound only, and when he got used to the little bandage I tied round his leg he became quite proud of it and displayed it to all and sundry: a habit which nearly got me into trouble with the Brigade Major, who, evidently disapproving of trench pets in general and bandaged kittens in particular, snorted at Scissors in an apoplectic kind of way which caused me great alarm. I knew that snort! I remember hastily asking a random question about gas masks, which happened to be his particular hobby, and the crisis passed.

'Thanks chiefly to a lavish diet of bully beef, which he adored (to the derisive amusement of the men in my machine-gun section) Scissors grew fat and fast. But he never forsook his nightly habit of rat-hunting. Rats in their thousands infected the trenches

When he's awake Smut helps to keep the mice away from the public library

A railway kitten named 'Midland' because of the M on her forehead

and dug-outs and gave Scissors plenty of scope. That most of them were larger than Scissors did not in the least deter him. Scissors discovered early in his life that a cornered rat will show fight and he was bitten several times in his nightly encounters. I can see him now, as the flare of the Verey lights used to reveal him, streaking along the trench boards in pursuit of a grey rat larger than himself.

'Poor Scissors! He was missing when the division moved to another part of the line, and there was no time to search for him. I often wondered what became of him. Somehow I cannot picture him as a casualty. I prefer to believe that he made friends with one of the officers or men who relieved us, or that he wandered across No Man's Land into the German line. My batman was horrified, I remember, at the mere suggestion, but I never had any qualms. If Scissors could survive the wrath of the Brigade Major he was safe enough with the Bavarians across the way.'

Our third professional cat enjoyed rather a soft time, but few pets have lived such a public life as Mike, the big tabby which for many years kept watch and guard at the gate of the British Museum in London. Day and night, summer and winter, for nineteen years, Mike was there with the gatekeeper, the policeman, and the tall liveried attendant whose scarlet collar and gold-banded silk hat declared his rank as King's Messenger — a reminder that when the Museum housed the private collection of King George IV the great Bloomsbury treasure house was guarded by the King's Guards.

Mike saw millions of visitors pass in and out, famous men and women from all the countries in the world, students, holders of readers' tickets for the famous Reading Room, American sightseers, Japanese and Indians, Australians and Canadians. The keepers told with pride how they had nursed Mike through the rigours of a particularly severe winter, when he was seventeen. They claimed that no scholar, visiting the Museum, could ever be quite as wise as Mike looked. He accepted life as philosophically as when, years earlier, he had abandoned all hope of ever killing one of the fat Museum pigeons that daily crossed his path. On hot afternoons the keepers closed the east gate and moved over into the shade of the

They also serve who only stand watch over the garden

west gate. Mike followed, but he was never happy there. Visitors saw him more easily at the west gate and with cries of 'Oh, Look! A pussy cat!' would stoop to stroke him, which Mike hated. At his usual gate, the one nearest Southampton Row, he had a way out, or rather up. Two leaps and he was safely esconced out of hands' way on the pediment over the lodge door. You can still see the place where the hard granite of the porch was worn smooth over the years by the impact of his feet and body.

As becomes all real professionals, he was a cat of means. When still a kitten he earned the respect of Sir Wallis Budge, then Keeper of Egyptian Antiquities. When the famous Egyptologist retired he still returned each week to contribute sixpence towards Mike's larder.

When Mike reached the ripe old age of nineteen he passed away into the same Unknown where, for 3,000 years his fellows in the Egyptian galleries of the Museum have resided. World famous, he was mourned by countless visitors. 'Where is Mike?' they asked, and the keepers shrugged their shoulders, and looked up at the empty pediment over the lodge door. Someone even wrote a verse about him:

> I scorned the public as it came
>   and went,
> To blandishments and fish in-
>   different,
> But sat for nineteen years and
>   kept the Gate,
> In every hair an Officer of State.

The amazing truth about Mike is that he never did a stroke of work in his life, probably never even caught a mouse, was well fed and lived happily, and yet was part of the Establishment. And that must surely make him the perfect professional.

Keeping birds from the fruit trees and rats from the barn

The Big Relatives

Cats are flesh-eating animals, and the larger members of the family bear familiar names — the Lion, Tiger, Jaguar, Leopard, Puma, Clouded Leopard and Cheetah. The smaller varieties include the Lynx, Caracal, Serval and Ocelot. The Leopard has the widest range of the big cats, being found throughout Africa and Asia, usually in wooded areas. He is even more savage and dangerous than the Lion or Tiger.

The Lion lives on the open plains of Africa and north-west India, but he is no longer common in India and in most countries he is protected.

The largest of all the cats is the Tiger, which has been known to reach a weight of 500 lb. Lions seldom weigh more than 400 lb, while fully-grown Pumas seldom exceed 180 lb. Like domestic cats, the larger varieties are solitary animals, hunting their prey silently, by stealth. They move fast in a short dash and pounce upon their victim but they cannot sustain speed. The Cheetah is probably the world's fastest animal, being capable of short bursts of up to 70 miles per hour.

All cats, from the Lion and Tiger down to your own pet at home, are similar physically. They are powerful, supple, and extremely agile. All except the Cheetah are provided with strong, sharp claws which have a remarkable retraction mechanism. You will notice that kittens claw at furniture or carpets or curtains to sharpen and clean their claws, and to keep them from growing too long. But they can be taught when they are quite young to use a scratching post or log in the garden or yard. Otherwise, your chairs will be ruined.

'Those who'll play with cats must expect to be scratched,' says Sancho Panza in *Don Quixote*.

Cats see best in semi-darkness and rely on their keen sight while hunting. Their sense of smell is less acute than a dog's, but they like the scent of flowers and herbs, especially catnip, lavender, wallflowers and roses. Lions and Tigers, of course, are said to be less particular.

The serval, an African cat which is prized by natives for its skin

The African Kaffir cat or fettered cat

Domesticated South Asian leopard-cat

A jaguar with her 3-month-old baby

The big cats can be tamed . . .

A toothy view of the genet, an African cat

The wild tigrine, or 'little spotted cat was mated with

. . . but they usually prefer the wild

an Abyssinian to produce the half-breed kitten shown below

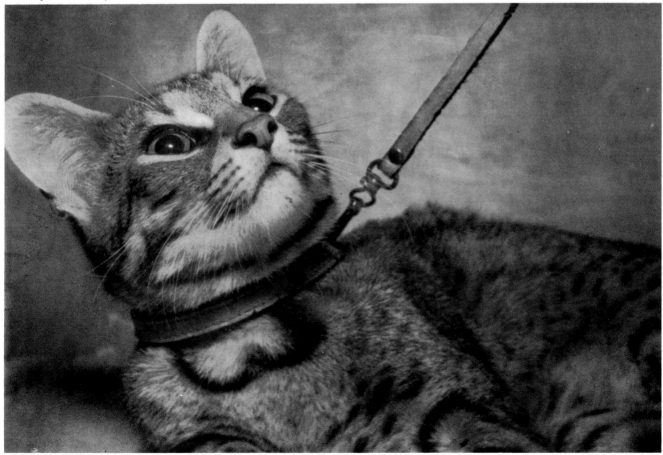

Wild Cats

The wild cat, *Felis silvestris*, lives in parts of central and southern Europe and parts of northern and central Asia. It is also to be found in France, and in Scotland. There is no doubt that it was once very common in Europe. It was the emblem of the Burgundians, and Clotilde of Burgundy, who married Clovis, King of the Franks in 493, bore a golden wild cat on her banner.

Although the Scottish wild cat was believed to be extinct at the beginning of the century it appears to have survived in the Highlands, where it is now reported to be multiplying rapidly. It looks like a domestic tabby but is heavier, the coat being a yellowish grey with black stripes on the flanks and a black dorsal stripe. The tail is thick, does not taper, and is ringed with black, the tip also being black. Wild cats breed freely with domestic cats but are fierce and tough. They make their home among rocks and cliffs as far away from man as possible. Wild cats on the west coast of Scotland have been known to fish in the sea for food.

Even though it is very small compared to the lions and tigers, the wild cat is just as intractible. Very few attempts have been made to keep it in captivity. Of these, only one or two have succeeded. Wild cats are very highly strung and simply cannot adjust to life in captivity. There are many problems: diet and infections, for example. But one of the biggest difficulties is this animal's savage and ferocious wildness. In Scotland, up till the end of the Middle Ages, the peasants were authorized to destroy them at will and use their fur for clothing. Scottish folklore is full of stories of these cat-hunts which turned into battles and which, in some cases, ended with the cat chasing the man back to his home. Many of these battles were said to be a fight, between equals, to the death.

There used to be a theory that the domestic cat was descended from the wild cat. Today we know this theory to be completely false. The domestic cat and the wild cat are two quite different species.

The Scottish wild cat may look like a big. domestic cat...

... but there is nothing domestic about its behaviour

Scottish wild cats are intractible and highly-strung

Therefore, very few attempts have ever been made to keep them in captivity

Scottish folklore is full of tales about battles between men and wild cats

The Manx

The short-haired tail-less Manx or 'Rumpy' from the Isle of Man is unique, although there are cats without tails in Japan and Malaya. Where the tail should start there is a hollow. Breeding the true Manx is difficult; they may produce kittens with long tails, kittens with stumps, or kittens without tails. The high back legs give the breed a walk which looks like a rabbit's hop. The hindquarters are high, giving the cat a curious appearance, the coat is short, and double, like a rabbit's fur, the head is large and round, and the ears are pointed.

The origin of the breed is a mystery. Legend says that the first Manx cats landed on the Isle of Man from two ships of the Spanish Armada wrecked off Spanish Point, near Port Erin. An old Manx newspaper says that in 1808 an 'East County ship was wrecked on Jurby Point, and a rumpy cat swam ashore'. Another tradition states that a Baltic ship wrecked between Castle Rushen and the Calf brought the Manx to the island. As the ship drew close to the shore two or three tail-less cats leaped from the bowsprit and were taken by the wreckers on shore, who were waiting for loot.

The explorer Auguste Pavie believed that the Annamite cats were connected with the Manx. The Annamites, small, graceful cats with very short tails, were probably imported into the East Indies from Britain by the trading expeditions in the eighteenth century.

An old Welsh legend states that Manx cats were known in Cornwall at an early date, and that it was from the West of England that the Manx went to the Isle of Man. They were evidently sacred animals, since they were said to have been the offspring of an ancient goddess.

Miss Mona Douglas, speaking to the Jubilee Congress of the Folklore Society in London in 1928, revealed that there was an old superstition in the Isle of Man that the cats have a king of their own. He is said to live the life of an ordinary house-cat by day, but at night he assumes his regal powers and travels the lanes in a fiery state. If the householder who

Manx cats can be any colour, but they can never have tails

owns the king of the Manx cats is unkind to his pet it is said that the king takes a terrible revenge. Miss Douglas added, 'Cats are believed to be on intimate terms with the fairies, and with all the inhabitants of the invisible world... and if a cat is put out of doors when the family retires, the fairies let it in again during the night.'

But perhaps the oldest and most amusing Manx story is the Biblical one. It seems that the Manx was the last of all the animals to enter the Ark. Noah was very impatient, because the waters were rising. But the cat was slow, so Noah hastened it along and hurriedly shut the door on its tail.

Said the cat, and he was a Manx,
Oh, Captain Noah, wait!
I'll catch the mice to give you thanks
And pay for being late!
So the cat got in, but oh,
His tail was a bit too slow!

The first Manx cat to become a champion in Britain is believed to be a silver tabby named Bunhalli, who was owned by a keeper at the London Zoo. The award was made at a show held at the Royal Botanical Gardens in the presence of the Princess of Wales, later Queen Alexandra, the consort of King Edward the Seventh. Louis Wain, the famous cat artist, was one of the judges.

High back legs are a Manx characteristic which sometimes produces a rabbit-like movement

Climbers

Most members of the cat family are expert climbers and will leap quite superbly with amazing agility onto the top of a wardrobe, an overhanging branch, or up a tree trunk. Firemen and animal welfare workers are constantly being asked to rescue cats from precarious perches from which they can't — or won't — come down. Cats often go too far and climb up to positions from which there is no easy way back to earth.

A few years ago a Swiss cat made headline news by climbing the famous Matterhorn. He was only a ten-month-old black and white kitten and he was the pet of the Hotel Belvedere (10,820 feet up) where every day he used to watch the alpinists set out onto the Hornli Ridge to climb the mountain.

One morning the kitten decided to follow a party of climbers and set out after them. He was soon left behind, but after a long and lonely climb he reached the Solway hut (12,556 feet). Early next day he started climbing again and when night fell he bivouacked in a *couloir* above the shoulder.

Next day he was seen by a group of climbers who passed him by, convinced that his climbing skill, if not his spirit of endurance, would be defeated by the difficult Ropes Slabs and the Roof. But they underestimated the kitten's ability, and some hours later they were surprised to see the cat, mewing and with his tail happily erect, reaching the summit (14,780 feet). Recognizing a gifted fellow climber, who had made the ascent without equipment or safety devices, they gave him a meal and took him down the Matterhorn and back to his hotel.

Cats are quite fond of high places —

whether roofs, window-sills or trees

Birmans

The Birman is the sacred cat of Burma and is very rare and valuable. There are few in Britain and fewer still in the United States, but their popularity is bound to grow. There are two varieties, seal and blue. Their points resemble the Siamese in colouring and they have white feet, a tiger-like walk, beautiful blue eyes, flowing coats and bushy tails. They are the aristocrats of the cat world.

It was in 1916 that a British army staff officer named Major Gordon Russell helped to quell a local rebellion in Burma and enabled a number of priests to escape into Tibet taking their sacred temple cats with them. There were over a hundred white cats living in the great underground temple of Lao-Tsun, where the priests believed that the faithful would return to earth after death in the form of cats. Lao-Tsun means 'the dwelling place of the Gods', and the cats who were born and lived there were worshipped by the priests and were treated like gods.

When Major Gordon Russell went to live in France in 1919 the priests sent him two of their sacred cats as a token of gratitude. Six years later the breed became officially recognized in France and Birmans began to win show prizes. Today the Birman is officially recognized in Britain and is unique among champions. The introduction of the breed from France is due to the energy of two London cat experts, Mrs E. Fisher and Mrs M. Richards whose beautiful Birmans are shown here.

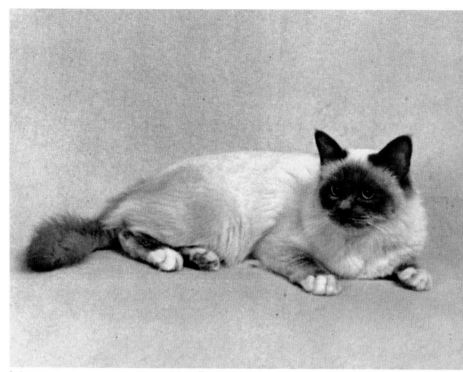

Orlamonde de Khlaramour, a Blue Birman

The first litter of Birmans to be born in England

Tabbies

Tradition says that the tabby gained its name from the district of Attabiah in old Baghdad where the Jews made a fine black and white silk with a watered effect. When this was introduced to Britain it was called 'tabbi' silk. The similarity between the stripes and water marks led to the cat being called the 'tabbi'. But many of the ancient Egyptian cats, as is shown by the drawings and models and mummies of earlier centuries, had tabby markings.

Tabbies are either striped or spotted and they range in colour from black to light cream or silver, and from deep chestnut (with copper eyes) to brown. Silver tabbies are more rare, the coat being of pure silver with distinct black markings but no breaks down the back, the markings being evenly placed on the legs and tail. The eyes are usually hazel or green.

Tabbies may be short or long-haired, with white or mackerel or spotted markings. Mackerel-striped tabbies have dense markings with narrow rings running vertically from the spine towards the ground.

Show tabbies must have neatly ringed tails and chests. The common ginger tabby in our back gardens and yards and alleys should not be confused with the darker red pedigree variety. But some of the most perfect pedigree cats have tabby markings which are no more attractive than those of Ginger — the cat next door. Old blood will out.

A long-haired Silver Tabby with distinct black markings

This Red Tabby has a long coat and a short tail

To many people, a 'tabby' is simply a cat. But it's the markings that make the difference

Many of the Ancient Egyptian cats had tabby markings. They might have looked like this elegant creature

A mixture of tabby and white

Going on Holiday?

Holiday time, which brings so much pleasure to millions of us, is often the occasion for unhappiness and suffering among household pets. Cats like companionship and are miserable when the family goes away. Too often they are forgotten in the excitement of going abroad. But a cat is unable to fend for itself and it needs proper arrangements for its welfare. If you are not sure what to do with your pet when you go away, here are some suggestions:

1. Arrange for a neighbour or relative to visit the house or flat every day to feed the cat and put out fresh milk or water and allow it to exercise, while making sure that it is securely inside at night.

2. Ask neighbours or relatives to look after your cat in their home. The risk here is that the cat may return to your house looking for you or its familiar surroundings.

3. Arrange for the cat to be boarded out in a cattery. Your local vet. or clinic or the nearest branch of one of the big animal welfare societies will tell you of a good boarding kennel.

Most big towns have catteries near them where cats may be boarded, but it is advisable to inspect the one you choose before you take the cat there. Make sure it is not over-crowded. The best catteries take only a limited number of boarders. A cat boarded out should first be vaccinated against feline enteritis. Take a note with you describing what food your pet prefers, and when you install him in his temporary lodging put a slipper or shoe or old sock into his quarters with him. He will recognize the smell of your body and he will be reassured that you have not forgotten him.

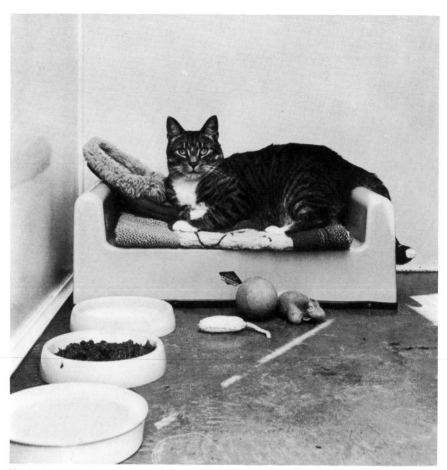

He isn't spoilt, he's just got everything he needs

If you take him away from home, he will need his own basket

What's So Funny?

It was that mad Cheshire Cat who immortalized the feline grin. 'He vanished quite slowly, beginning with the end of the tail, and ending with the grin, which remained some time after the rest of it had gone.'

But most cats are happy to stick around and have a good laugh at their own jokes.

Take Fluff, for instance, who is shown at right. This three-month-old kitten has an excellent reason to smile. She has just spent two days inside a refrigerator. How she got in is a mystery, but when she was rescued she was just a bundle of ice. A place in front of the fire and a bowl of warm milk soon melted the ice and brought on the smiles.

A cat doesn't have to have a reason to wear a gay expression. Rex, an Abyssinian shown below right, may have just heard a shaggy dog story. Or perhaps the photographer has asked him to say 'cheese' or watch the birdie.

Everyone knows that cats can't really giggle or guffaw, but anyone who has ever had a cat will recognize the 'laughing look' on the faces on the following pages.

Whatever it was, it was enough to make a cat laugh

And this is the one who had the last laugh

The Post Card Cats

In its long span of existence nearly everything has happened to the cat. He has in turn been worshipped, held to be the devil, been sacrificed in the name of religion or superstition, and at various times has been believed to be both lucky and unlucky. It was only in the nineteenth and twentieth centuries that the cat at last emerged as a harmless, attractive domestic companion, although even now, at least in Britain and most Commonwealth countries, cats are still not protected by law.

Today the cat is generally considered to typify domestic harmony, the happy family around the fireside. If a black cat crosses your path in the morning, you will have a good day. Few people now regard white cats as unlucky, as they once did. In the modern world of smart automobiles, gracious living, and instant meals, the cat has become associated with thick, warm carpets and luxury goods, and is an emblem of stability and success. He is a status symbol, appearing on cigarette packets and sweet cartons, while the beauty of his figure has attracted the postage stamp designers of Poland, the Yemen, and Czechoslovakia.

Tabbies and Persians and short-haired Whites help to sell clothes, refrigerators, blankets, and big boxes of chocolates. Who can resist buying a 2 lb. box of soft centres with a blue-eyed white kitten on the outside? Cats appear in Walt Disney cartoons (all descended from the famous Felix the Cat made immortal by Pat Sullivan), and sometimes they even steal the picture from such accomplished actresses as Audrey Hepburn or Hayley Mills. Strange to think that in medieval times the same cats would have been brutally treated.

The change in public opinion can be traced from mid-Victorian times. In about 1860 people began to experiment in producing different varieties, and pedigrees were gradually evolved. The idea of a cat sitting by the fireside fitted in well with the Victorian ideals of domesticity and family bliss. The great Queen liked cats and it was no coincidence that Lewis Carrol introduced a kitten that turned into a Queen — and back again — in *Alice*

One of the most famous kittens in the world

Through the Looking Glass. Towards the end of the Victorian era there came a boom in cat pictures, cards and calendars, with Louis Wain and his many imitators enjoying tremendous popularity with their sketches.

In Europe and the United States the cat became emancipated at about the same time as the picture post card craze started. The habit of sending post cards, at first for only a halfpenny, usually from seaside resorts, grew towards the end of the century until, by the outbreak of the 1914 war, it had reached gigantic proportions. Tens of millions of picture post cards flooded through the post offices of America, Britain, Germany, France, Scandinavia and Italy. Actresses were great favourites and in Britain photographs of the famous Dare sisters, Ellaline Terriss, Gladys Cooper, and the Gaiety Theatre beauties were sold in millions. There were also sentimental pictures, often with verses, and in many of these there appeared cats or kittens, usually sitting in floral baskets or with children, and often wearing coloured bows. Sometimes the cats were drawn as humans, wearing the fashions of the time, but usually they were photographed simply looking pretty. The cards were not only tokens of good luck, they were symbols proving that everything was well with the world in those peaceful, prosperous days, when you could travel from London to Brighton for 3s. 9d return, hats in the ladies' department stores at $1/1\frac{3}{4}$ d and $2/1\frac{3}{4}$ d each were knocked down to $6\frac{3}{4}$ d each, there were still many more horse-drawn vehicles than there were horseless-carriages, there were less than ten miles of concrete roads in the whole of the United States, and beer in London cost two shillings for a dozen pint bottles.

For a few pence you can still buy these old cards in second-hand shops, junk stalls, and street markets. You will find them in the back-streets of London, the flea market in Paris, the side-streets of New York and Chicago and the Jude Market in Amsterdam. They may be slightly thumbed these days, but you will find most of the post marks are dated between 1903 and 1914. That is, after the Boer War and before the great conflict, in the carefree Edwardian

Alice's kitten turned into a queen in *Through the Looking Glass*

era. Once the great European war came, there was a spate of photographs and sketches of soldiers saying good-bye, or making jokes in the trenches.

The sentimental tidings on the old Edwardian cards usually wish some-one good luck or a happy birthday or a merry Christmas, but the scrawl-ing on the back is often faded and rather sad. Who knows what hap-pened to all the kittens who posed for these pictures, or indeed to all the young men and women who hastily scribbled a few lines to send home before setting out along the prome-nade to listen to the military band, in the summer sunshine of long ago?

Very lucky with the weather. Wish you were here. Back on Sunday night. Love from Gladys and Tom. Today the messages are similar but the pic-ture post card business is not quite the same. Sentimental cats have given way to big, coloured photographs of the New York skyline, or Venice by night, or the Tivoli gardens in Copen-hagen, or the Arc de Triomphe from the air. But the old post cards are still there if you trouble to find them among the bric-a-brac and second-hand books, in the corners of our cities. There the Edwardian pussy-cats stare at us, representing a way of life that has changed, and a lost generation.

Louis Wain, photographed about 1890 with one of his models. He began a cat vogue that continued with the photo postcard

GLAD BIRTHDAY WISHES

I WISH YOU LUCK, I WISH YOU PLEASURE,
AND HAPPINESS IN ENDLESS MEASURE,
I WISH YOU JOY I WISH YOU HEALTH,
AND ALL YOU EVER NEED OF WEALTH.

W.E.K. 686.

The Victorians believed that cats brought good luck, and cats soon came to be emblems of all sorts of good wishes

What's for Supper?

He will seldom bite the hand that feeds him

Opposite: Sit up and beg

Cats may be curious to try whatever is on the table, but they're better off with their own diet

The Rex

Although domestic and show cats are divided into two types, long-haired and short-haired, there is a third variety. This is the Rex cat, whose fur is short and dense, the hairs being wavy instead of straight, with the coat looking curly.

The Rex is comparatively rare, there being less than a hundred in Britain, the result of special breeding. The kittens are curly from birth and can be of any colour. Rabbits have also been bred with the same curly coats, but Rex cats have only one coat layer, unlike ordinary cats, which have three — a soft undercoat, a middle coat, and guardhairs.

They are affectionate, intelligent and extremely hardy. Even the whiskers curl. But because there are so few of them, they are very expensive. It is said that the Rex can easily be trained to walk on a lead.

The Rex is a relatively new and rare breed

Many people think they have a beauty all their own

The Rex can be any colour, as long as their coats are curly

The pussycat with the permanent wave. Many people call them 'poodle' cats

Cat-Nap

'A nap my friend,' wrote George Bernard Shaw, 'is a brief period of sleep which overtakes superannuated persons when they endeavour to entertain unwelcome visitors or to listen to scientific lectures.' Mr Shaw knew a great deal, but cats know better. It is said that Winston Churchill put his feet up every afternoon, and enjoyed a cat-nap. No doubt he learned the art from his marmalade tom. Given a warm corner away from draughts or a place in the sun, most cats will doze off.

It is Sancho in *Don Quixote* who has the last word on sleep. 'God bless the inventor of sleep,' he says, '...the cloak that covers all men's thoughts, the food that cures all hunger...the balancing weight that levels the shepherd with the king and the simple with the wise' ...and the cat with the man. It is pleasant to imagine that the great Churchill dozed in front of the fire, with his friend enjoying a cat-nap by his feet.

The great thing about being a cat is that you can go to sleep anywhere

Yawn!

Persians

Snow White, a white Persian

Long-haired cats first arrived in Europe at the end of the 16th century when the naturalist and explorer Nicholas de Peirese introduced the Angora cat into France. Angoras later became known as Persians and are now generally called Long-haired. Their distinctive features are their long flowing silk coats, a ruff around the neck which extends and mixes into the long hair around the head, and small ears set well apart. The nose is snub and broad, the legs are short, and the tail is short but full and fluffy. Long-haired cats are to be found in a variety of colours, although the Blacks are rarer than they used to be. Long-haired Whites, which usually have blue eyes, are the original Angoras or Persians, but most blue-eyed cats are deaf or have poor hearing. Some of the loveliest Persians have orange eyes, and are not affected by deafness.

Perhaps the most popular of the long-hairs is the Blue Persian, accepted as a pedigree breed in Britain since 1898 and very highly prized in the United States, France, Germany, Scandinavia and the Commonwealth countries. But Long-haired cats may also be Cream coloured, Red, Smokey, Silver Tabby, Brown Tabby, Red Tabby, Chinchilla, Blue-Cream, Colourpoint, Tortoiseshell or Tortoiseshell-and-White. The Long-haired Tortoiseshell, like the Short-haired variety, is well-known in most countries. Most of them are females, and those which are males are usually sterile. The Colourpoint, with its cream coat, dark points and mask, and blue eyes, combines the coat pattern of the Siamese breed but is certainly not a Siamese. It is in fact unique, and was not officially recognized until 1955, although it is today one of the most popular breeds.

Long-haired cats need more grooming and attention than the Short-hairs, but their owners say that they repay all the time and trouble which must be lavished on those long, silky coats. Perhaps there are not so many of them as there are short-haired cats, but they are certainly the aristocrats of the cat show world.

A cream Persian with a determined expression

Show cats Jewel of Dunesk and Pauline Pullen

Fanta of Culloden, a champion Blue Persian

Do Cats Hate Water?

Watch a cat staring at a dripping tap or faucet, see how he gazes at a pool in the garden, and you will realize that he is strangely attracted by water. Anything that moves — an insect, a mouse, a bird — makes him curious. But flowing water provides a special attraction, even in the bathroom. And although cats are not noted swimmers, simply because they dislike getting wet, are delicate, and catch cold more easily than most animals, there have been many instances of cats who really *like* swimming, even in the sea.

One cat which likes a regular dip in the ocean and loves yachting, is an Australian mouser named Tippy, the household pet of Mr and Mrs R. J. McDonald of Beauty Point, Mosman, New South Wales. From the moment that daughter Jan brought Tippy home from school, their pet was a natural sailor.

Mr McDonald started it all by building a 31-foot ocean racing sloop in his backyard, and as Tippy saw the *Saris* taking shape she decided that the yacht would be her special home, a refuge from neighbouring dogs, with a pleasant deck where she could lie in the sun and watch the family.

When the *Saris* was launched, Tippy decided to go along too. After all, it was her home. So Mrs McDonald made her a lifejacket. But of course the only time Tippy went overboard by mistake she wasn't wearing it.

At first Tippy was reluctant to get even the tips of her paws wet, but now she happily scoops fish out of a bucket of salt water and even leaps ashore from the ship's dinghy, completely unafraid. One day she dived overboard when the *Saris* was about fifty yards from the shore. In her own independent way she had decided it was time to go home, and set out bravely swimming for the landing. The McDonalds were alarmed, because Middle Harbour is full of sharks. But while the family became entangled in fishing lines and mooring ropes in their frantic efforts to rescue her, Tippy paddled on towards dry land, and made it. Then, when she had reached the shore, she calmly sat down and began drying herself. Who says cats don't like water?

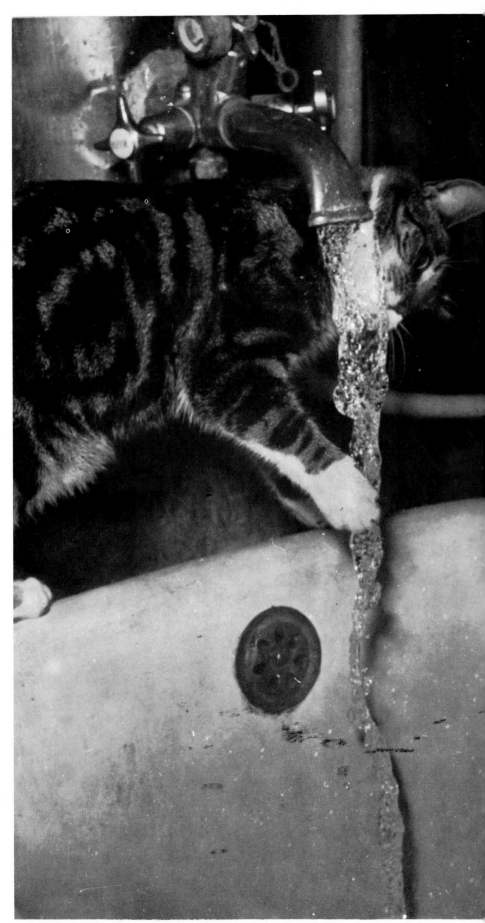

Anything that moves — especially water — fascinates them

Jan McDonald and her Australian swimming cat Tippy

Cat's Company

People who don't own cats sometimes ask 'Do cats get on well together? Aren't they always fighting?' You might just as well ask the same questions about humans. No two cats are alike, some are quarrelsome and others are docile and good-natured. But most cats like feline company and if they are brought up together they will stay together happily. A lonely kitten is sad to watch, but a kitten among his brothers and sisters is full of energy and games. See how cats wash one another, and curl up together for warmth and company, and you may wonder what Rudyard Kipling meant when he wrote 'The Cat. He walked by himself, and all places were alike to him'. Kipling was more attracted to dogs than cats, and he must have failed to observe how well most cats get on together and how much domestic cats like human company, as well as the companionship of other cats.

When cats disagree or fight it is usually because a tom cat has encroached on another male cat's territory. They are suspicious of strangers, two-legged and four-legged, and undoctored males often fight simply to gain possession of a beautiful female. But most cats, especially at home, are perfectly content to sit close to one another purring contentedly, especially if they know that each has a separate eating bowl and a particular place in their owner's affections.

A cat that walks by himself

Come outside, the weather's fine!

I always like travelling by tube

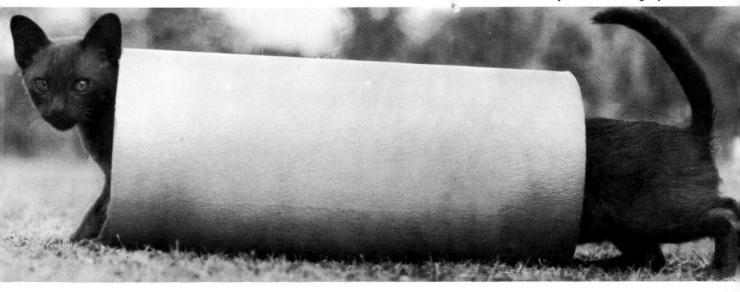

There's nothing like a friend for warmth and comfort

On a Cat, Ageing

He blinks upon the hearth-rug,
And yawns in deep content,
Accepting all the comforts
That providence has sent.

Louder he purrs, and louder,
In one glad hymn of praise
For all the night's adventures,
For quiet, restful days.

Life will go on for ever,
With all that cat can wish:
Warmth and the grand procession
Of fish and milk and fish.

Only — the thought disturbs him —
He's noticed once or twice,
The times are somehow breeding
A nimbler race of mice.

Alexander Gray

'Life will go on for ever,
With all that cat can wish...

One in the hot Italian sun — and one in the shade

Ten Golden Rules

If you own a cat you have responsibilities which cannot be neglected, but they are not arduous. An unhealthy cat is a misery, a nuisance to neighbours, and a source of infection to other animals. On the other hand, a cat that is loved, well-fed, carefully groomed and kept under proper control, is a companion who will spread happiness.

A cat will demonstrate his happiness in a number of ways, notably by purring and holding his tail aloft while waving the tip from side to side, or by rubbing his body against your legs. Sometimes he will show his affection by giving you a lick on your face or ear or hand — a kiss of affection.

Your cat's requirements are very few. All he or she needs are:

(1) A comfortable sleeping place away from draughts.

(2) Two varied meals a day, or one, according to the size of the meal. But if he is a kitten he will need more, smaller meals.

(3) Fresh water or milk in a bowl

(4) Exercise and fresh air

(5) Daily grooming

(6) Human companionship and understanding

(7) The company of another cat if possible

(8) Some control of his or her sexual activities

(9) A permanent home with people he or she has learned to trust, who regard their pet as one of the family

(10) The services and advice of a qualified veterinary surgeon in times of sickness, that is, an M.R.C.V.S.

A fine cat deserves fine care

A lively kitten is always a delight

But who can doubt the more permanent, more mysterious appeal of the cat?

Acknowledgements

We would like to thank the following people for permission to reprint copyright material: Hughes Massie Ltd for Paul Gallico's 'Doors' from *The Silent Miaow*; Souvenir Press Ltd for the extract from George Freedly's *Mr Cat*; Sir Alexander Gray for his poem *On a Cat Ageing*.

The author's 'Ten Golden Rules' were originally published in *Looking After Your Cat* by Allen and Unwin.

Every care has been taken to discover the owners of copyrighted material, but if necessary acknowledgements have been omitted, we trust the copyright-holders will accept our apologies.

Author's collection. 114 B, 115 (2)

Barnaby's Picture Library. 27 TR, 30 B, 37 B, 40 B, 84 T.

Black Star. 23 (2), 25 (2), 27 TL, 32, 47, 56, 58 B, 59 T, 68, 69 T, 76, 77, 80 (2), 100, 119, 129.

Jane Bown. 63, 85 T, 89, 120 (2), 121, 122 (2), 123 (2), 125 T, 134.

British Museum. 18, 19 T.

Jane Burton. 91 T, 91 BL, 92 BL, 93.

Camera Clix. 58 T, back jacket.

Camera Press. 20 B, 34 TR, 36, 42 T, 44 (2), 45, 46 T, 59 B, 69 B, 73 L, 87 T, 88, 90, 92 T, 101 L, 106, 124 T, 133 T.

James Carr. 84 B.

Central Press Photos. 62 B.

C. Connolly-Smith. 55 TR.

S. N. Dalton. 82.

Clayton Evans. 15 T.

Reginald Eyre, at Photo Centre. 26 B, 38 B, 118 B.

Patrick Coyle. 75 B.

Mrs. E. Fisher. 102 T.

Fox Photos 74, 98 B, 99 B, 127 T, 127 B.

Will Green. 22 (2), 27 B, 31 T, 40 T, 43 T, 51, 57, 72 B, 73 R, 81 (2), 83, 101 TR, 101 BR, 110 T, 111, 123, 126, 138, 139.

Paul Hamlyn Library. 112, 113, 135 T, 136.

Claude Harris. 20 T.

E. O. Hoppé. 21 B, 29 B, 35 TR, 35 B, 43 B, 52 B (2), 53 B (2).

Keystone Press Agency. 13 B, 14 T, 16 TL, 54 B, 71 B.

Luciana's Photos. 15 B, 16 B, 17.

Kevin MacDonnell. 116.

K. J. Mierendorff. 130.

Photo Illustrations. 94 (2), 95 (2), 96, 97 (2).

Photo Researchers. 54 T.

Pictorial Press. 19 B, 41, 105 B.

Paul Popper. 24 B, 28, 42 B, 46 BL, 46 BR, 52 T (3), 53 T (3), 55 TL, 55 B, 60 T, 65 T, 71 T, 72 T, 79 B, 92 BR, 93 B, 109 (2), 117, 125 B, 135 B.

Press Association Photos. 91 BR.

Radio Times Hulton Picture Library. 12 T, 14 B, 16 TR, 64, 114 T.

R.S.P.C.A. 34 TL, 67 (2).

Sport & General Press Agency. 60 B, 61 T, 65 B, 66, 110 B.

W. Suschitzky. 21 TR, 26 T, 33 (2), 34 B, 38 TL, 38 TR, 39, 79 T, 104, 105 T, 124 B, 128, 140, front jacket.

Syndication International. 11 (2), 30 T, 50, 61 B, 62 T, 86, 87 B, 102 B, 108 (2), 127 C, 133 B.

Sally Anne Thompson. 98 T, 99 T.

Topix. 13 T.

Roger Viollet. 12 B.

Frank Woods. 21 L, 24 T, 29 T, 70 (2), 85 B.

Nicholas Wright. 10, 31 B, 35 TL, 37 T, 48 (2), 49, 58 B, 75 T, 78, 103, 107, 118 T, 131, 137, endpapers.